CASE OPEN

Also by Harold Weisberg

CASE OPEN
The Unanswered JFK Assassination Questions

Harold Weisberg

A Richard Gallen Book
Carroll & Graf Publishers, Inc.
New York

First Carroll & Graf edition 1994

Carroll & Graf Publishers, Inc.
260 Fifth Avenue
New York, NY 10001

Library of Congress Cataloging-in-Publication Data

Weisberg, Harold, 1913–
  Case open : the unanswered JFK assassination questions / Harold Weisberg.
  — 1st Carroll & Graf ed.
   p. cm.
  ISBN 0-7867-0098-X (pbk.) : $11.95 ($16.50 Can.)
  1. Kennedy, John F. (John Fitzgerald), 1917–1963—Assassination.
 I. Title.
 E842.9.W36 1994
 364.1'524—dc20   94-7011
                            CIP

Manufactured in the United States of America

Publisher's Preface

As the FBI testified in open court, no one knows more about the assassination of President John F. Kennedy than Harold Weisberg.

Case Open is a book Harold Weisberg felt compelled to write. He felt the need and determination to set the record straight. Written with a blinding passion and brilliant analytical skills, it raises serious questions about the methods and integrity of Gerald Posner's *Case Closed*. He examines the process in which a book so dishonest can be published with such fanfare and with such little regard for verifying the evidence it presents. *Case Open* is a simple yet complete rebuttal of Posner's book.

Weisberg demonstrates that Posner's main thesis is misappropriated research of a highly questionable nature. Posner has suppressed, distorted and omitted evidence and misled the reader into believing that he has developed new evidence and promoted the concept that he had sponsored the scientific computer enhancements.

Weisberg, a former OSS and United States Senate investigator, wrote and published *Whitewash* in 1965. It was the first book to seriously question the conclusions of the Warren Commission. Today it is still regarded as one of the seminal works of research on the assassination. He has since written and published many books and articles on the assassination.

In the 1960's and 1970's Weisberg fought many landmark freedom of information battles that effectively established today's basic Freedom of Information Act. His personal files on the Kennedy assassination run into many hundreds of thousands of pages. Gerald Posner used these files in conducting three days of research at Mr. Weisberg's home.

In the process of proving that Posner has in actuality proven nothing, Mr. Weisberg exposes another sordid chapter in our nation's greatest enigma, the assassination of John F. Kennedy. Case Open.

Preface

When President John F. Kennedy was killed in Dallas, Texas, on November 22, 1963, I was liquidating a promising poultry farm that had been ruined by low-flying helicopters. I had filed one suit for the damages my wife and I suffered and in winning a small award established a new legal principle, that the property owner owns the air space above his property to the height required to enjoy his constitutional right to own property. When even the secretary of defense could not end the harassment by helicopter, he directed his general counsel to look out for our interests and to negotiate a settlement with us for subsequent damage. It was pursuant to this agreement that I was engaged in an orderly liquidation of what I, along with many other soldiers in World War II, had dreamed of: being free and independent by becoming a farmer.

What does one do when in middle age he has to make a new start? I decided to return to writing. I got an agent and was researching a book in which I hoped to do to noise what Rachel Carson did to chemicals: alert the country to the great suffering and damage from noise. Then the President was assassinated on the streets of a modern American city, and I—like most Americans—spent every minute possible before the tube and when doing my chores had a transistor radio on my belt and an earphone in an ear to keep up with the news. I read the papers with care, too. With each new report I became more concerned about all that was happening that should not happen.

From my background—and I am not a lawyer—I could not see how an impartial jury could be picked. I also could not see how any of the alleged evidence was not already tainted. Within two days I did not see how the lone accused, Lee Harvey Oswald, could be tried. After the second round of tending our flocks and gathering eggs, sitting before the TV with my after-breakfast coffee, I told my wife he was going to be killed. My thinking was simple: all that was being done was making it impossible to try him; someone wanted to close his mouth, and the only way to really do that was to close it permanently—to kill him.

Because I never expected it to happen where it happened, and as it happened, when I saw it happen live on TV, I may have been more shocked than anyone else because I *had* expected it . . . but not on camera, and not in police headquarters.

When I proposed a magazine article on the assassination to my agent I lost my agent! She was quite explicit in telling me that nobody in New York was considering or would consider anything other than what the government said.

I then abandoned the book in which I had hoped to alert the country to the great dangers from noise. I decided to do what I had done professionally; analyze the official report on the assassination when it was issued. I had been a reporter; an investigative reporter—a United States Senate investigator and editor; first as a soldier and then as a civilian, I had been an intelligence analyst, beginning in the OSS, the Office of Strategic Services.

General William ("Wild Bill") Donovan, the conservative New York lawyer who headed the OSS, enabled me to get off to a good start there. Awaiting me, after my security was cleared, based on my prior investigative experience, was a lawyer's job in which the lawyers had failed. Donovan was an old-fashioned military leader. He believed he owed responsibility to those under him.

Four brave young men who had volunteered for a parachute drop in France behind Nazi lines, an assignment from which survival was not very promising, had gotten into a fight with the military police in a Washington suburb. They had been convicted and all appeals having failed were serving their time at Fort Tilden, New York. Donovan did not believe they were guilty. The lawyers having failed were, he decided to have a nonlawyer take a shot at it.

Without any investigating at all, without even going to the scene of the crime, by analyzing the records in the case made by the lawyers, I found what they had missed, and six weeks after I began, turned in the report that freed those four men. It gave me quite a reputation among those who knew about what I had done, and thereafter, although my work remained analysis, I was used as a troubleshooter. Other components bounced to me what they could not handle. Not a single one of those assignments turned out to be difficult, when approached differently.

One that I recall was even from the White House, with a forty-eight-hour deadline. By not missing the obvious that counterintelligence had missed, I finished that one in a morning.

When I learned that political Neanderthals in the government were about to cause unpleasantness for the radio station on which I was the news and special events editor over my nonexisting past, matters of which I was innocent and in all instances exonerated, I decided the time for implementing that soldier's dream of freedom and independence had come.

Farming promised to be a radical change from the kind of life I'd led, with none of that kind of challenge. No Nazi cartels and their interference with the war effort to investigate. No secret history of OSS operations to write and have stolen, despite its classification, and appear as a Jimmy Cagney movie, *O.S.S.* No articles based on my own research, like one for a minor magazine that became another movie, one that put a new phrase in our language, "Gung ho!" No labor spies and strikebreaking murders like those of the 1930s to look into as part of my work for the Senate.

The peaceful clucking of contented chickens is what I looked forward to.

I bought a tract of abandoned farmland at the northwestern end of the Montgomery County, Maryland, village in which my wife was raised. It had not been farmed since the end of the previous century. With only hand tools I cleared the land and began to build. That heavy physical labor is one of the reasons I am still alive at eighty.

In the age of increasing mechanization and mass marketing, we turned the clock back. I delivered what we raised to the consumer. We sought and achieved greater quality and in a small way became famous in our field. My wife became the national chicken-cooking champion; I became the national barbecue king and we won first and third prizes in the whole country for raising chickens.

Our customers ranged from receptionists and janitors in Washington offices to the top in Washington political and diplomatic life. Two were then cabinet members, one a former cabinet member, and we served embassies and ambassadors. Those who relished our birds ranged politically from the former Dominican dictator, Rafael Trujillo, to Winston Churchill. When Mrs. John Foster Dulles, wife of the secretary of state, entertained Mamie Eisenhower, she selected our birds to serve. Bertha, the Dulles's cook, told me the next week that Mamie had gone down to the kitchen to learn where she had gotten such fine birds. When Lady Knox-Monroe, wife of the New Zealand ambassador, entertained during the organization of the Southeast Asia Treaty Organization, she also served them, and the next week Rosie, her Austrian refugee cook, told me—as Bertha had—of the reception they got.

That so promising a business could be ruined simply because helicopter pilots violated regulations and disobeyed orders—and a special order had been issued to avoid our farm by a six-mile circle—was a learning experience. It was painful and costly, but it certainly told me that what is not supposed to happen can and does happen, despite the efforts of the secretary of defense himself to end it.

Having saved all the locally available newspaper accounts of the assassination and its investigation and recognizing most of those stories as leaks, when the President's Commission Report was issued on September 27, 1964, I went to the Government Printing Office where I had spent so much time beginning when I was in my early twenties as a Senate editor, arranging for the publication of our hearings and reports. I bought three copies of that Report; two in paperback and one hardback to keep, not to use in working. I began reading and analyzing it as soon as I had driven home. Two months later, when the Commission's twenty-six-volume appendix was issued, I was there again and bought two sets, one to work with and the other to preserve.

In 1992 I gave that mint set—still in the sealed cartons—to Hood College, a fine, small college in Frederick, Maryland, the town where my wife and I have lived since the liquidation of our farm and where all my records will be a permanent and free public archive.

I began with a book contract under which I was to deliver the manuscript by February 15, 1965. I mailed each chapter as I finished it. And I did finish it on time, although that was only five months after that report was issued and only three months after the twenty-six-volume appendix was published. When I went to New York City a week or so later to see the publisher, he was drooling into the till from the advance sale of about 39,000 without a word of advertising or promotion, merely from the salesmen mentioning the book to booksellers. Then the vice president of that publishing house which soon, deservedly so, went belly-up, told me one night about this promising advance sale, and the next morning went to Washington. He returned after that one-day trip, the contract was broken, and I did not even get the manuscript back! No explanation, just the rejection and nothing else. That was the first of more than a hundred international rejections, without a single adverse editorial comment for the very first book on the official investigation of the assassination of a President.

What a shock it was, particularly because of my background, that the first book on so important an event—the assassination of a President—could not find a publisher!

After all those rejections, although broke and in debt, I was able to publish *Whitewash: The Report on the Warren Report* myself. I had to become a publisher to open that subject up for national discussion based on the facts in the book, the first on that Report. Without a cent for advertising or promotion I made a success of it. In all it went through thirteen printings. Dell, which rejected it three times, decided to reprint it after I made a success of the original edition.

Dell's first printing was of 250,000 copies. It reprinted three more times. Although I became probably the country's smallest publisher (I probably remain the country's smallest publisher), after twenty-nine years there is still a demand for that book. Because of my age, eighty, ill health, and a medical prohibition against lifting more than fifteen pounds, I can keep it available only with a special xerox edition of it. It remains the basic book on the subject and is used as a text in several colleges and universities. And, twenty-nine years later, I have not had a single factual criticism of it or a single complaint from anyone mentioned in it, or in any of my six subsequent books alleging unfair treatment.

To me, what I report above represents one aspect of the failure of our basic institutions, beginning with the government and including book publishers and the major media. It still seems incredible that with as significant an event as the assassination of a President, the first book on it could not be published commercially.

When the Freedom of Information Act (FOIA) was enacted in 1966 to become the law of the land the next year, I began using it to bring to light suppressed assassination records. Although as the result of thirteen FOIA lawsuits I obtained about a quarter of a million previously withheld pages of government records, mostly those of the FBI, and including those relating to the assassination of Martin Luther King, Jr., a total of about a third of a million pages, the courts also failed. They did not require the government to abide by FOIA. The Congress recognized this when in 1974 it amended FOIA to restore the congressional intent when that law was enacted, the intent changed by the government in judge-shopping to produce decisions it wanted contrary to the intent of that law. One of my first suits, for the results of the scientific testing in the JFK assassination, was misused that way. In the debates in 1974 amending it, it was the surviving Kennedy brother, Senator Edward Kennedy, who saw to it that the legislative history would be explicit in reflecting that my suit was the basis for the amending of the investigatory files exemption of the act that opened FBI, CIA, and similar files to access under it. (*Congressional Record,* May 30, 1974, page S9336).

Perforce my work on the assassination and its investigation also became a study of how our basic institutions work, or failed to work, in that time of great stress and ever since then. In my *Never Again!* which is being prepared for publication as I write this, and in this book my examination of the failure of publishers is more explicit. That is because in *Never Again!* I examine the intrusion into these political matters by the *Journal of the American Medical Association (JAMA)* and the major media's treatment of those articles that got such widespread attention, and in this book I do that with Gerald Posner's mistitled *Case Closed* and his publisher, Random House, and the help with that commercialization and exploitation by the major media and the CIA.

Because I believe that FOIA bespeaks basic American belief, that the people have the right to know what their government does, I believe also that the information I obtained by those lawsuits is not mine in the sense that personal property is mine. I therefore make all that information available to all writing in the field even though I know that almost all will write contrary to what I believe. As it turned out, unexpectedly, Posner was not an exception.

When the first of a series of complications following major surgery in 1980 and then more complications after other major surgeries—the last of which was open-heart surgery in 1989—left me incapacitated I was as a practical matter virtually denied access to these records, many file cabinets of which are in our basement. I decided that with the knowledge I have acquired in this work that the best use I could make of the time that remains to me, happily more years than I had hoped for after my 1975 hospitalization for circulatory obstructions, is to perfect the record for our history to the degree possible for me. I have made no public comment on almost all the books with which I disagree, books I regard as commercializations and exploitations of the great tragedy, but I have annotated the most successful of them for history's record.

Analyzing *JAMA*'s incompetent and factually grossly incorrect exploitation in defense of what I regard as the official mythology of the JFK assassination did not require my use of those basement records. This is because the searching and refiling were done for me by a fine young woman who was a prelaw student at local Hood College, Helen Wilson. Her part-time work was invaluable. It was made possible by my friend Richard Gallen. That enabled *Never Again!* to include what she retrieved from my files that otherwise would not have been accessible for me.

But in writing this book I am not able to make much use of those records because Helen graduated. It is ironic that from the three days he and his wife spent here, Gerald Posner had more direct access to my records than I have had.

In neither *Never Again!* nor in this book is anything I say intended personally.

Author's Note

Posner's small-minded effort to diminish my work and question my character has the effect, to those who really know the subject matter and the work done in it, of making himself even smaller.

The minor detail he selected from all my work to allege is inaccurate, distorted and, as what he presents as the fact, grossly in error.

In some of his criticisms of me, he misrepresents what my books were about in order to contrive an entirely irrelevant criticism.

He knowingly misrepresents what he knows to be the truth to accomplish his dishonest and disreputable objective, which is to defame me and to question my character.

As he well knows in his little-man dirtiness, there is nothing that can be done to remove from the minds of his readers the character assassination he intended.

But that does not and cannot make him any larger than the small man he is.

Posner boasts of his 200 interviews. In fact he uses them to circumvent the established *official* fact his book cannot survive. A writer of integrity checks to determine whether a source is dependable. Posner's most prized sources are not.

Basic to Posner's book is his claim that Oswald was a born assassin, waiting for his moment in history, for his time to assassinate. His sole claimed source is Dr. Renatus Hat Hartogs, the psychiatrist who examined Oswald as an unhappy, delinquent little boy. But in the very Warren Commission testimony Posner cites on the very page under oath, Hartogs swore to the exact opposite!

Who is this shrink? One who was found in court to have used his women patients for free sex. As Posner would have found in my files had he checked Hartogs at all.

Posner singles out the expatriot Cuban Carlos Bringuier for special praise and thanks as a source. If he had consulted my file of FBI records on Bringuier he would have learned that he is not dependable as a source and has inflated notions of his importance. He actually expected the JFK assassins to assassinate him and wanted the FBI's protection! (Posner says Oswald was the lone assassin.)

Hubert Badeaux is another of Posner's prized sources upon whose word he depends. There are many disqualifications of Badeaux as any kind of source Posner would have found when he was here he had any interest at all in being truthful, accurate of dependable in his book. Badeaux distributed literature describing the respected conservative Democratic Louisiana Congressman Hale Boggs, who was also a member of the Warren Commission, as a Communist!

Posner had free and unsupervised access to all the *official* information I have when he worked in my files and copied whatever he wanted. These are but a few samples of what he did not want to know because, had he known it, he would not have any book at all.

With pettiness and factual error, he criticized those with whose writings he disagrees. The truth is that each of his contrived criticisms lacks honesty of intent and of expression. In this, he has characterized himself for the record for our history.

In terms of the nature of his criticisms, to which he seeks to give an importance they do not have, in personal terms they are worth no more time and space than the categorical statement that they are all in varying degrees dishonest and he knew it when he wrote them.

For the record for history, for scholars of the future, there is a much longer, detailed and documented manuscript in my files copies of which will be deposited with several universities.

". . . I remembered reading of your pro-bono FOIA work on behalf of Harold Weisberg. I respect his work, and know he has fought some staggering battles. . . . I am interested in contacting Mr. Weisberg and getting some guidance from him regarding my project. . . ."

(From a letter dated January 20, 1992, from Gerald Posner to James H. Lesar).

". . . I appeared on Fox Morning News with Gerald Posner sometime in November. After the show he took me aside and told me, 'Look, I know the case isn't closed. . . .'

"After the Fox show, I appeared with Posner on an Irish talk show by telephone. This was probably a week or two after the Fox show. During the course of this show I noted that Posner had told me that he knew that the case is not closed. Posner did not dispute my statement. . . ."

(From a letter dated January 4, 1994, from James H. Lesar to Harold Weisberg.)

CASE OPEN

I

Gerald Posner's Road to Glory

All hail Gerald Posner!

He has done the impossible—what had not been done in thirty years! He solved the JFK assassination case; what the Warren Commission, the FBI, and CIA, and all those other government agencies—and all the others who have written on the subject (which for almost all means more or less on the subject)—those Posner criticizes and condemns throughout, were not able to do. Thus, with his characteristic modesty, his title: *Case Closed.*

All the major media seem to agree. There was virtual combat to get him on the tube. Even the CIA pitched in by arranging for its prized and secreted KGB defector, Yuri Nosenko, to appear with Posner on the August 27, 1993, *20/20.* Tom Brokaw had him on NBC. Even Marina Oswald, who for years had disagreed strongly with Posner's *Case Closed* solution, that alone and unassisted her late husband did it all, helped him. The Oswald daughter, June, was on TV with him right away.

Media notables were so excited in advance of publication that they jeweled the dust jacket with virtually unprecedented praises.

David Wise heralded it as the long overdue "voice of san-

1

ity''; as ''brilliantly researched . . . utterly convincing and compelling.'' Frederick Dannen (author of *Hit Men*) proclaimed: ''This book really does close the case.'' Displaying his detailed and intimate knowledge of the writing in the field, Dannen is ecstatic because Posner, ''for the first time ever, presents an account of the Kennedy assassination devoid of speculation.'' (Did he read the book?)

Apparently William Styron did not read Dannen's hosanna because he says Posner's analysis is ''a brilliant and meticulous analysis,'' and one man's ''analysis'' is another man's ''speculation.'' Stephen Ambrose is a bit cagier, although he does conclude that ''This case had indeed been closed by Mr. Posner's work.'' (Saying it is *his* work is worth remembering.) Ambrose must have read one of Posner's earlier books, perhaps *Mengele,* or had one of Posner's earlier books in mind speaking of *Case Closed* as the work of ''a single researcher, working alone.'' Posner himself, in the half of his dedication about his wife Trisha says she is his ''partner'' and two are not ''a single researcher.'' In describing the book as ''a model of historical research'' Ambrose was apparently so overwhelmed by Posner's representation of what he had done and read in little more than a year that he did not even ask himself if that were possible for ''a single researcher.'' All those interviews, all that travel, all that reading of so very many books, with ten million words in the Warren Commission's twenty-six volumes of appendix alone besides its 900-page Report, and indexing that massive appendix too. Referring to all of this and the time of the writing as a mere ''model'' of the work done in not much more than a year by a single man falls far short of an adequate description of the impossible.

Tom Wicker begins his encomium referring to all the literature on the subject, as does Posner, as of ''one Kennedy assassination conspiracy after another,'' which both know not to be true, refers to them all as ''dishonest,'' a word that will come back to haunt, and concludes, ''the case of JFK is indeed closed.''

The publisher broadened it a bit, adding ''the Warren Commission erred.'' Perhaps not without reason Random House does not include the FBI and the CIA. But it does begin its pitch without false modesty and unequivocally by saying that "After thirty years, *Case Closed* finally succeeds where hundreds of other books (considerably fewer than Posner's imagined two thousand books) and investigations have failed—it resolves the greatest murder mystery of our time, the assassination of JFK."

What Random House and Posner say comes from the "latest scientific and computer enhancements of film and evidence" in fact comes from something else; something not at all new.

Random House quotes Stephen Ambrose on the back-cover blurb: "Mr. Posner's chapter on the single bullet is a tour de force, absolutely brilliant, absolutely convincing." We'll see.

Random House singles out as new "startling details from his (Oswald's) classified KGB file" as it does in referring to some of the book's Oswald content as "told for the first time by the KGB agent who handled his case." This is not true. ABC-TV News had access to that same supposedly "classified KGB file" and broadcast it months before the book appeared and that former KGB agent (former by almost three decades) did not "handle" Oswald's case. His importance is that he knew about it and for a short period of time after the assassination had and read the "case" file when it was retrieved from Minsk for that agent, Yuri Nosenko, who then was based in Moscow.

There is no "revelation" in the book that Posner got from Nosenko, who was a gift to him from the CIA, as he does not tell his readers and for which he paid with his integrity.

What Posner used from the KGB is not quite in accord with all those ecstacies of wonderment resplendent in the blurbing.

His "brilliantly researched" book, David Wise's words, "meticulous," William Styron's "model of historical research," Stephen Ambrose's, and "deliberate, detailed, thoroughly documented," Tom Wicker's, does not include "KGB" information I published in 1975. And Posner has that book.

Returning to those "secret files" in Random House's claim, and to what Posner learned, thanks to the CIA from "the KGB agent who handled his case," perhaps no more than the usual publisher falsity and excess in referring to Nosenko, Posner's book says that Oswald and Oswald alone was the assassin.

Nosenko disputed this, telling the *20/20* audience he shared with Posner that Oswald could not hit the side of a barn door with a shotgun, let alone a rifle, and could not have been the assassin.

What Random House refers to as "the latest scientific and computer enhancements is the key, in Posner's own words (pages 321–2), to his new "solution" to "the greatest murder mystery of all time, how he and he alone "closed" the case. This gets to Ambrose's "tour de force"—Posner's proof of the single bullet theory that is quintessential to the official "solution" to the crime and to Posner's, and to a sweet little (then ten-year-old) girl, now married and a schoolteacher.

Posner attributes his new evidence that "closes" the case to "New Zapruder enhancements."

Abraham Zapruder was a Dallas manufacturer of women's clothes. His place of business was on the third floor of the Dal-Tex Building. It is across Houston Street at Elm, on the northeast corner of what is called Dealey Plaza. On the other side of Houston Street at Elm is the Texas School Book Depository building (TSBD—since taken over by Dallas County), in which Oswald worked and from which Posner says Oswald fired the three shots of the assassination, as do the official accounts of the crime. (That of the FBI and the Secret Service are not identical with that of the President's Commission appointed by President Lyndon Johnson to investigate and report on the crime, known after its chairman as the Warren Commission. The fact that there are mutually contradictory official solutions Posner does not trouble his readers with.)

Zapruder, standing atop a concrete structure to the west of the TSBD building, used a Bell & Howell eight-millimeter motion picture camera in photographing what became the most important single piece of photographic evidence of the crime and the official time clock of it. Motion pictures are really a series of individual pictures called "frames." That film of that era was only about 5/16 of an inch wide.

Zapruder assigned his rights to his film to the Time-Life

publishing giant. It provided 35-millimeter color slides of some of the film's frames to the Commission. Enlargements of some of those frames were made for the Commission by the FBI laboratory. They became Commission Exhibit (CE) 885, published in the Commission's Volume XVIII of those twenty-six volumes of appendix, on pages 1 to 85, inclusive. (18H1–85). They are published two to a page. As I brought to light in the second of my six published books on the JFK assassination, *Whitewash II: The FBI-Secret Service Coverup* (1966), for an unexplained reason the commission failed to publish the last nine of those frames of this exhibit. As the result of my exposing this, those slides were added to the trays of them in the National Archives in Washington where they can be projected, reviewed, and studied, as I did in 1966 and early 1967.

The Archives is the repository for all disclosed official assassination records. Before long, bootleg copies of Zapruder's film, most of poor quality, appeared and were themselves duplicated. Posner does not tell his readers any of this, perhaps—but not necessarily—indicating a rush in the writing and editing of his book for appearance before it was scheduled to appear. He also does not say what copy of the film he says he had enhanced, whether it was the original that, after scandals about the film and the extraordinarily high charges made for its use, Time-Life returned to the Zapruder estate. It deposited the film in the Archives. Because Zapruder's heirs retain the copyright, Posner and Random House required their permission to use any version of that film. The more remote from the original the copy of the film used, the greater the loss in clarity.

When motion picture film is projected for viewing, those individual frames are moved by a sprocket whose teeth engage rectangular holes cut into the film when it is manufactured.

What Posner also keeps secret in his "deliberate, detailed, thoroughly documented," and "conclusive" book is that a little more than 20 percent of the image captured in the film is not seen when the film is projected or when it is duplicated in automatic copying machines. Keeping this secret is an absolute essential to Posner's interpretation of what he says is the "enhancement'' of the film that is the basis for his ''closing'' of the ''case.'' In any honest examination of the film, its meaning and the timing of the shooting, this 20 percent of the image that is lost when the film is projected is also an absolute essential because it holds quintessential evidence not seen on projection.

This relates to 35-millimeter still pictures taken by a bystander, Phil Willis. When he took the fifth of the series of his pictures in the commission's evidence, it is established beyond question in the image that exists only in that part of the film not seen on projection. I brought this to light in my second book in 1966. It has not been contradicted, and Posner has that book. Posner raised no questions about it with me. I obtained about a quarter of a million pages of once-withheld official records, mostly those of the FBI, by a dozen lawsuits against the government under the Freedom of Information Act. In them, there is no contradiction of what I had previously published.

This timing is a vital element in any version of the ''single bullet theory.'' It is as unquestionably vital to Posner's book and ''solution'' as it was to the Commission's. Both ignore it. Neither makes any mention at all of it. This, too, is what Ambrose refers to as ''a tour de force, absolutely brilliant, absolutely convincing.'' It *is* a tour de force, but not the kind Ambrose imagined, as we shall see.

This illustrates the hazard to those of prominence who know nothing at all about a subject yet are unstinting in their praises of the work of any author when the personal and professional integrity of the endorsers is the captive of the personal and professional integrity of the author. The endorsers are limited to what they read in the book and what they read in the book is what the author wants there. They have no way of knowing whether the author includes all that is relevant or even if he is truthful.

Posner does not say when or for whom or for what purpose his ''enhancements'' were made. This leaves it to be wondered if they were not made for him, as he implies they were.

Most of this ''enhancement'' Posner attributes to Failure

Analysis Associates in a note beginning on page 317, and extending on to page 318. He describes what it did as "an extensive undertaking involving 3–D scale generations (sic) of Dealey Plaza, physical mockups of the presidential car, and stand-in models for the President and Governor, all to determine trajectory angles and the feasibility of one bullet causing both sets of (nonfatal) wounds (to both victims)." Failure Analysis also recreated experiments with the 6.5 mm ammunition, using more updated information than was available to the Warren Commission, to further test the "single-bullet theory" and the condition of the missile.

One thing only is clear about Failure Analysis: Posner does not say this elaborate and costly work was done for him. However, his writing is carefully designed to give the impression that it was done for him. The prestigious *Philadelphia Inquirer,* a major newspaper that has won many Pulitzer Prizes, praised him for going to all that trouble and expense. But Posner was careful to give that impression without actually saying he paid for that work and that it was done for him. He also does not say in his book that claims to "close the case" of the Kennedy assassination, who invested such an extraordinary amount of money in an effort to prove that the single bullet theory was valid and then gave it all to him, without any charge. Is it right for Posner to keep the identity of Failure Analysis's client secret? . . . or the reason for this very big undertaking?

Why *does* he keep it secret? He dares not even give an address for Failure Analysis, or say how it is staffed. There are, as we shall see, many questions about this book, but perceiving most of these questions requires detailed knowledge of the facts of the assassination of President Kennedy and its official investigations and of the literature.

There are also many obvious questions: obvious to the kind of critical reading those asked to endorse a book ought to have been expected to do before vesting their reputations, or risk having their reputations misused to endorse a book that deceives and misleads the people; one that, as Posner undertakes to do, has as a purpose, writing his version of some of our history; one that, as Posner does not hide, has as a purpose defaming others.

All these many people of influence abdicated their responsibilities to the public, to themselves, and to the country. They recast themselves as mere propagandists. Posner himself discloses that he personally made no such effort that decent, honest, and responsible writing requires.

These are but some of the many questions that are obvious in any critical reading of a thoroughly bad book, a professionally and designedly dishonest book. But of all the many questions and mysteries, none cried out as loudly for attention as Posner's obscuring of where he got what. Without it, he has no book at all.

Should not any mature mind have wondered why he makes a mystery of why Failure Analysis for all that costly work and, if he did not pay for it, what right he had to use it or how he got it?

Should not the obviousness with which he makes a mystery of it not have raised additional questions, the most basic questions when, without it, he has nothing but a diatribe that in itself should have raised questions?

There is also the mystery that is in itself a commentary on what has happened to our major media, to those who let the people know what is happening in their lives and to their country; why not one of these men of outstanding reputation asked a single question about the work done by Failure Analysis or its purpose—even whether Posner's is an honest representation of it. As it is not.

All those reviewers, reporters, and many TV and radio people also should have been other than propagandists and should have asked this same and other obvious questions as well. Nothing more was required than a phone call to Failure Analysis, or to Posner or his publisher, Random House. Yet there is no indication that any one of these professional communicators did that simple thing.

Well, there is no mystery about it, other than why all these many communicators failed to meet their personal and professional responsibilities, as in due time we shall see. And, in seeing this, we shall also see that among the many communicators, some of whom are paid more than highly paid corporate executives, there was not one with the perceptiveness of the little boy in the fable who told the emperor his garments of fabulous beauty did not exist and that he was naked.

This raises still another question: What does all this say of the state of the "fourth estate," of the nation, and of its future?

II
Posner's Nitty-Gritty Grits

The Kennedy assassination part of Posner's book ends on page 342. It is followed by his Jack Ruby story. But not until ten pages before the end does Posner get into his nitty-gritty, that fabulous enhancement of the Zapruder film, available to him alone, and the basis of his vaunted "closing" of the "case" of "the greatest murder mystery of our time," Random House's lighthearted description of what was known as "the crime of the century," the crime that turned the world around, that most subversive of crimes that subverted our society and nullified our system of government.

He gets into his great discovery saying, "Beginning at (Zapruder) frame 160, was a young girl in a red skirt and white top who was running along (sic) the left side of the President's car, down Elm Street, began turning to her right. But by frame 187, less than 1.5 seconds later, the enhancement clearly shows that she has stopped, twisted completely away from the motorcade, and was staring back at the School Book Depository. That girl was ten-year-old Rosemary Willis."

Posner's wording reflects the Wall Street lawyer in him as the writer; there is no trick too petty or too dirty to pull on his reader to seem to make his point. The Willis girl, as he well

11

knows, was *not* "running along the left side of the President's car." She was not near it. The President's car was in the middle lane of the street that had three lanes painted onto it. She was to the President's car's left, but she was neither close to it nor in the street. She began on the paved sidewalk on the south side of Elm Street. That sidewalk ends not far from Houston Street and all that side of Elm Street from there to the west is then grass, until close to the coming together of three streets, from the south, Commerce, Main, and Elm, to funnel through the triple underpass that carries a wide expanse of railway tracks over the merged streets.

Rosemary Willis was never "running alongside the President's car" and Posner knew that very well. After all, did he not have that fantastic "enhancement" right before him?

Posner's gross and prejudicial misrepresentation should not divert attention from the fact that he says that it is clearly and exclusively from those "new Zapruder enhancements" one can see the girl has stopped . . . and was staring back at the depository building." Without his enhancements, he says, this would not be known.

This is what Posner says he and he alone "uncovers" in his book, and only through "the latest scientific and computer enhancements of film . . ."

After saying that Phil Willis's little girl stopped because her father called to her (to which we shall return), Posner says that was not the reason: "However, when Rosemary Willis was asked why she had stopped running with the President's car, she said, 'I stopped when I heard the shot.' "

At this point Posner has a note numbered "18." His notes at this point tell so much—about him.

Continuing, nothing omitted in quotation, Posner gets to his keystone, what supports all of his solution to the crime, what is new, thanks to the enhancement and to him: "The Zapruder film is the visual confirmation that provides the timing." This "timing" is *his* timing; *his* proof that the first shot fired (he says), was the one that missed, and that it was fired at about frame 160, not the frame 210 that—despite Posner's denial of it—is basic to the official "solution." He then, still nothing omitted in quoting, has another quote: " 'In that first split second, I thought it was a firecracker. But within maybe one-tenth of a second, I knew it was a gunshot ... I think I probably turned to look toward the noise, toward the Book Depository.' "

Who Posner quotes here he does not say. It is not the Willis girl. Ten year olds are not likely to be able to understand what "one-tenth of a second" is. Posner, instead of telling his readers who he is quoting, has his footnote "19" here.

He resumes, still nothing omitted in quoting, "Just after Rosemary Willis slowed and started turning toward the Depository, the enhanced film shows that President Kennedy was waving as the car turned the corner and suddenly stopped waving."

I skip further quotations of this because it means nothing at all, as anyone who has ever suffered the embarrassment of being the one honored in a motorcade, as for Miss New Jersey Blueberry Queen, or, as I was in 1959, the "National Barbecue King," knows, one has to wave all the time, except when, briefly, the arms are rested, and it does get to be a terrible bore. However, Posner is careful not to identify what he refers to above keyed to the only timing device, that Zapruder film each individual picture of which was given its official number by the FBI agent: Laboratory Agent Lyndal L. Shaneyfelt.

Posner continues: "In addition to the reactions of the Willis girl, the President, and Mrs. Kennedy, Governor (John B.) Connally's recollections and actions confirm a shot was fired before frame 166." (Page 322). Whoa, Nellie! (Which happens to be a phrase as well as Mrs. Connally's name.) Didn't Dannen say Posner's book is "devoid of speculation?" And isn't Posner's *speculation* about those "recollections and actions" his only "confirmation" of that early shot in those magical "enhancements" for which a fortune was paid by his benefactor whom Posner does not identify?

Anyone familiar with the Warren Commission testimony of which Posner makes only infrequent mention knows that Posner gives it his own interpretations, and to which he naturally gives the meaning he wants it to have rather than what the witnesses are known to have actually meant. What Posner really says boils down to that one ten-year-old Willis girl and the meaning he gives to her actions from that computer enhancement and from nothing else.

With this, Posner says that from one of Governor Connally's motions, "beginning at frame 162, when the Willis girl started turning around and the President stopped waving," is when that first shot was fired (page 322).

I return to what I skipped for continuity in what Posner says about the "enhancements and the Willis girl" that he broke the continuity to say—that is, to his little distraction about one of his "somes." It turns out to be one and not "some" when Posner said that "some" believed the girl had stopped running because her father called to her. "Some" is evidence? . . . not the "theory" Posner supposedly never resorts to? It lacks the slight validity that can be given to a theory. Posner's note for this is on page 553. It reads: "17. Interview with Jim Moore, March 9, 1992." The average reader has no way of knowing whether Moore is an authentic expert or an assassination nut. He is a nut, but he happens to believe, as Posner does, that Oswald was the Lone Assassin. That is enough for Posner, who can find few kindred souls. So he treats Moore not like the nut he is and pretends this is a dependable, quotable "source."

Jim Moore's book, *Conspiracy of One: The Definitive Book on the Kennedy Assassination,* Fort Worth, Texas, the Summit Groups, 1990, 1991, is in Posner's bibliography, (page 582). Doesn't sound much different than *Case Closed,* does it? . . . "The" definitive book?

Posner sure can pick 'em. Real dependable people like all those big-name plugs say.

When Moore was a high school kid in Knoxville, Arkansas, in 1975, he called himself, "The John F. Kennedy Assassination Research and Documentation Center." He sent me a copy of a story about him in the *Arkansas Democrat* for July 26 of that year. He was a farsighted youngster, humble and modest, too. He once wrote to me that he planned not to take his high school senior year so he could graduate college in an election year, when he then could run for President of the United States.

Posner theorizes, in open defiance of the existing, proven official evidence, although "speculates" would probably be closer. There is no basis in fact for his argument that Oswald was on that sixth floor at the time of the assassination or for his speculation about the time of Oswald's departure from it. What Posner says is much like what Moore says in his chapter "At the Depository: The Physical Evidence." In that chapter Moore, (apparently seeking fame other than as President of the United States), recounts the evidence he and his friend and helper Rick "discovered" when they got permission to remove the plywood floor that was being laid over the very hard and very tough old flooring on the sixth floor on the day of the assassination. They were looking for proof about how the cartons of school books had been stacked in that alleged sniper's nest.

Attributing special importance to the arranging of those boxes is typical of the genius of those who defend the official solution, no matter what! Nobody knows how those boxes were stacked at the time of the assassination as we shall see later, if indeed they *had* been stacked in any particular way. They had been moved from the other side of the floor where they had been for the new flooring to be laid as Posner knew, if not from his "diligent" research of the Warren Commission records then from page 33 of my *Whitewash: The Report on the Warren Report*. Citing the Commission's own evidence (21H643) and testimony (7H1401) I showed that those boxes (allegedly making up the "sniper's nest") had been moved by the police as soon as they reached that point in their search. I also published four of the Commission's photographs that also show what the testimony proved (pages 204–5). But nothing as insignificant as established fact deters those determined to prove Oswald the lone assassin.

Like Posner, what Moore goes for, Moore finds. This is what makes him so fine and authoritative a source for Posner. In his reconstruction, after lifting the new floor off, Moore says (pages 44 and 45) they found that the "marks on the old wooden" floor from the alleged sniper's nest of the alleged stacking of cartons "were again visible when we removed the plywood to prepare his exhibit." They had to have been marks made the day of the assassination . . . "since there was no way for those marks to move during the 25 years they were covered over . . . they serve as extremely accurate guides for the placement of the boxes for the exhibit.''

Now, because that is what Moore *wanted* those alleged marks could not possibly have been made by anything else during those many years of many stacks of cartons during the decades of that building's life. Because he required for his own fame and glory that cardboard boxes at one time only made "marks" on that tough old seasoned hard wooden floor, by golly, Moore found those marks! And those marks only! Yup. Posner knows how to pick 'em, the most dependable of sources!

Moore's absurdity not only didn't keep Posner away from him, Moore did not draw a cutting remark from Posner as did each and every author who did *not* agree with the Warren Report. Posner used Moore as a source when there was no reason to use him! Posner wrote (on page 238), "Those who study the Plaza (Dealey Plaza) are not surprised by its usual echo characteristics." Anyone really familiar with the Warren Commission testimony could have found a source to cite in the official information. And almost anyone is a more probative "source" than Moore! Posner's note for this is on page 542: "Moore, *Conspiracy of One*, page 22. "There is no book more ridiculous for Posner to have used as a source! But Posner seems to want to mention Moore. What else did he cite Moore for? For Moore's use of Commission testimony: the very testimony Posner presents himself as expert on: "Counsel (Joe) Ball then asked (Lee) Bowers if he had familiarity with the sounds coming from "two locations in the area. Bowers replied he . . . had noticed at the time the similarity of sounds occurring in either of these two locations. There is a similarity of sound because there is a reverberation which takes place at either location." (Page 33.)

Posner in his argument makes a big thing about ear witnesses. In addition to citing Commission testimony, Moore also says on that page, "Again, the Plaza is a vast echo chamber."

From Posner's own representations of his own most diligent scholarship in the Commission's published information, Posner had no need for citing Moore. For example, in his fourth note in his Chapter 14, Posner uses a very generalized and essentially meaningless note; meaningless if a reader wants to check that source for himself: "Author's review of witnesses' statements published in the 26 volumes of the Warren Commission and available at the National Archives."

In itself this is an unusual statement. Those twenty-six volumes were published. While they are rare, they are still available secondhand, more rarely new, but they are and have been available. Why this reference to the National Archives? Are they not also available in numerous libraries, like Posner's own New York City library?

On July 12, 1992, I wrote to Posner, needling him a bit: ". . . Jim Moore wrote someone who gave me a copy of a letter in which he says, 'Vincent Bugliosi (Los Angeles prosecutor in the Charles Manson case and a strong, uninformed, and vociferous supporter of the Warren Report), apparently agrees with me [that is, Moore], and a book by Gerald Posner (sic) will be published by Random House in 1993 asserting that my solution is indeed the correct and valid reconstruction of the crime.' Thought you'd be interested." I did not dream for a minute that Posner would take Moore seriously. Moore's overweaning ego is apparent in his letter, that those with bigger names agree with *his* "solution."

Posner replied under date of July 16: "Received your note of June 12 and found it amusing. If I knew what I believe in this complex area, I certainly would not be working so hard as I am to make some headway through boxes of documents and piles of interviews." This was also to tell me that Posner had not yet decided what he believed about the case. The evidence is that he began with a preconception and published what he began believing. The notes on his interviews leave this without any question at all. So does his conduct and what he was and wasn't interested in when he was here in February, 1991. He did not ask me for evidence in support of Oswald as the lone assassin or for evidence against it. If Posner read Moore's book and read that nonsense about box prints and then looked him up, that says all that need be said.

Posner continued: "I met Mr. Moore when Trisha and I vis-

ited the Book Depository during our trip to Dallas a couple of
months past. He seemed like a likeable fellow ... I am not
sure how I can agree with his 'solution' to the case. Everybody
sees what they want to see.'' (Posner is not an exception!)

Posner's use of Moore as a source and that strange source
note so general in nature and indicating to uninformed readers
that he studied those twenty-six volumes at the Archives suggest
that all Posner's work was not his own, and that he in fact is
not as familiar with the extensive and available information as
he pretends to be in his book. He hadn't much more than a
year in which to do all his traveling, interviewing, researching,
reading and writing and, as we shall soon see, much more. It
simply is not possible for any one person to have read all the
sources he cites, and, where he is critical, as he is of almost
all writers other than Moore, he had to read more of his books
than the passages he criticizes, to be fair and not to err. Without
reading the entire book, he could not know this.

It is not impossible that those he trusted gave him much of
the passages he quotes and how to criticize them. There are
agencies with such interests and facilities. From the many thousands of FBI pages I received in those FOIA lawsuits, it became
obvious that the FBI has just this kind of operation, and an
extensive one, in the division it called ''Crime Records.''

Among the nonpolice, noninvestigative roles those agents
played was putting together entire books for writers the FBI
knew would welcome and would write what the FBI wanted
published. The FBI had its favorite writers and publications too,
and it used them effectively to manipulate and control the news
and what people could know and believe.

From its own disclosed records, the CIA was quick to do
that and to support the Warren Report, not a normal function
of intelligence agencies. It's first target was Mark Lane when
he traveled abroad.

The CIA did Posner an enormous favor, first giving him
something almost unique and then what was entirely unique in
promoting his book: it made its prize KGB defector, Yuri Nosenko, available to him. Nosenko can be reached only through
the CIA. The assumed name under which he lives and where

he lives are believed to be essential in keeping him from being killed. Of this truly rare favor done him by the CIA, Posner says (page 502): "Only twice before had Nosenko agreed to private interviews, and they had not been about Oswald. A journalist from one of the earlier meetings had later disclosed the state in the U.S. in which Nosenko was living, forcing him to move. Despite the risks in granting another interview, he agreed with the argument of my first letter to him, emphasizing his duty to the historical record. The extended time he spent with me, combined with his recall for details, was more than I originally expected."

Hogwash! Nosenko agreed to the interview because the CIA told him to grant it and the CIA would do that only if it was absolutely certain of Posner and of what his book would say.

Bearing on this is what Posner has in his book that he attributes to Nosenko. It is frills for the preconceived writing; no more. It is certainly less if there is interest in the assassination and about the real Oswald and what the KGB thought of him than was readily available, for example, in my *Post Mortem*. It dates to 1975.

There is more, much more that was published in book form and available in libraries. There also was the sensational nationwide telecast of one of the most sensational congressional hearings of all time. But as Posner knew, people forget. It is not clear that the famous writers and the historian who plugged this book before publication both knew and forgot about that hearing in reading Posner's book?

Yet, even after interviewing Nosenko who was already on the public record, saying the exact opposite, Posner says that Oswald had a rifle in Russia and became proficient in its use. What Nosenko told the FBI is that with a shotgun Oswald was so poor a shot that when he went hunting his friends gave him game to take home because he never once hit an animal.

Moreover, as Posner should have known, private ownership of rifles was then prohibited in the USSR, and certainly the officially approved hunting club of which Oswald was a member would not have permitted rifles—if any had been available. But they were not.

We return later to what Nosenko told the FBI that Posner had and did not use. His reasons for not using it are highly suggestive.

There is a further strong suggestion that Posner's book is unofficially *officially* supported. Nosenko's agreeing to be interviewed at length, even after his life was considered endangered by the previous interviewer, was truly exceptional. Posner's was only the third interview Nosenko granted in his twenty-nine years of secret living in the United States.

His public appearance for the very first time on *20/20* with Posner, even with his face hidden, is not less than remarkable and unprecedented. Why in the world should Nosenko have traveled to the New York studio just to promote a book with which he then disagreed so publicly in saying that Oswald was not and could not have been the assassin? As of course he would have told Posner in the interview—if Posner had cared, or been honest enough to ask. But that would have endangered his book with its preconception that had to be at the least known to the CIA for it to arrange for the Nosenko interview.

There certainly is no question about it; nobody about whom the CIA is not absolutely certain can even get a letter to Nosenko, let alone interview him, and then have him for the first time ever come out of his secret life to promote a book on nationwide TV. There are ample indications that Posner paid the CIA back and that it knew he would. One example is Posner's not using the readily available information from Nosenko that was already public. The quid pro quo is painfully obvious to all who are informed and not blind in the mind.

One of Posner's acknowledgments—on the same page (502) as his thanks to Nosenko but separated from it and in a sentence that has no apparent connection with it—is to the CIA: "A special thanks to both Cynthia Wegmann, Esq. New Orleans, who allowed me to review her father's voluminous papers on the Garrison case, and to Peter Earnest, chief of the CIA Office of Public and Agency Information who was always generous in his assistance." *Always?* In more than making Nosenko just *available?* In connection with "the Garrison case?"

That "case"—except to government agencies like the CIA

and the FBI—was not "the Garrison case"; it was the Clay
Shaw case. New Orleans district attorney John Garrison had
charged Shaw with conspiring to kill JFK. He had so little
evidence that the jury, which believed there had been a conspiracy, found Shaw not guilty in less than an hour. There were
unproven allegations published abroad that I reported in *Oswald
in New Orleans* that Shaw was CIA. (page 248).

Why does Posner have these unusual formulations, unusual
for a writer and unusual for a lawyer, referring to Edward Wegmann's records of his defense of Clay Shaw, one of whose
defense counsel he was, not as the Shaw case but as the Garrison case? And why does he bracket this with the CIA by thank-
ing both in the same sentence?

Why, too, should Cynthia Wegmann have trusted Posner and
been certain that he was writing a book in accord with her
father's beliefs? What kind of assurances could he have given
her and from whom that would have persuaded her to grant
Posner that also unique favor?

It was when I came to Posner's writing about the Willis girl
and the "enhancement" basis for his book that I decided to do
this writing, and began it. Among the reasons is that *it is the
entire basis for the book; that little girl and those "enhancements"* and how Posner handled it. Up to this point which is
only a few pages from the end of the assassination first part of
Posner's book, I recall no use of any record that seems to be
from or is attributed to the CIA, and I am certain that in his
notes Posner cites not a single thing he got from the CIA. Why
then does he bracket his thanks to the daughter of Clay Shaw's
chief defense counsel with his thanks to the CIA official with
whom he dealt and to whom he attributes not a single record;
and why that "always generous in his assistance" when there
is not a single citation of any information as coming from the
CIA's public office and when his book reflects not a single
record coming from that office or from that agency?

What dybbuk crept into Posner's mind and snuck into his
computer when he wrote this?—especially when there is no
question about the fact that Posner could not possibly have done
all the work he uses and cites in the time he had for this

book. For his single Nosenko interview, if Earnest arranged that
"always generous in his assistance" is not an appropriate
formulation.

Then there is something else that is strange. Posner knew I
had done much work on Oswald and he should have known that I
also had done much on Nosenko. I forecast more writing on
both in what I published and he had. If he looked at the labels
on my many file cabinets, with which he spent three days, he
would also know, if he didn't know earlier, that I filed two
Freedom of Information Act lawsuits to obtain the results of
the FBI's testing of JFK assassination evidence. That he is a
lawyer may not have led to his knowing that the first of those
suits led to the amending of the act's investigatory files exemption to open to FOIA access files of agencies of the CIA and
the FBI. But as it is well known and reported in the field and
with minimal research, he should have known about it. He
makes as big thing later about some of that evidence. Yet when
he was here, he asked me nothing at all about it. He had free
access to sixty file cabinets of information yet he did not ask me
for or about any Oswald, Nosenko, or test-results information.

Posner also had (as did all writing in the field always have
here) free and unsupervised access to the third of a million,
once-secret official pages I received after a dozen difficult and
costly and long-lasting lawsuits under the Freedom of Information Act. Some of those suits lasted more than a decade. The
case records alone fill more than two full file cabinets. The CIA
refused to let me have, even in lawsuits, information about
Oswald and other materials that were to be given to the people
under that law. But it gave Posner access to Nosenko. Posner
and his wife Trisha spent three days here copying whatever
they wanted, and my Nosenko information is quite voluminous.
They did not ask for it. Trisha's account is that they made 724
copies on our copier. It is not more than obvious that with its
consistent record of compelling those it knew did not agree
with the official "solution" to the crime to sue for information
it then still withheld that the CIA had to be certain in advance
of what Posner's books would be and say?

Another indication in the book that can possibly relate to the prized "assistance" Posner got from the CIA is a source note on page 511: "Based on interview (sic) with confidential intelligence sources (sic)." Those are never possible without official approval, if not arranging.

It is clear that at the very least the CIA knew from the beginning that Posner's book would be to its liking.

Disclosed CIA records also make it clear that the CIA's researches include precisely the kind of information Posner uses throughout his book, especially on and about writers. That is one possible explanation of how he could cite so great a volume of work and sources far beyond the capability of the fastest traveler and speed reader to travel to, locate, read, record, and then cite in the time he had before he began writing the book.

The normal time spread between the handing in of a manuscript and the publication of a hardback book is six months. Posner's book was on sale before the last week of August, 1993. Posner told me he was just beginning his work in February, 1992. And what a truly great amount of work he refers to, cites and claims to have done! Yet he had only about a year or a little more for everything, including the writing.

There is only one way of explaining this: much was given to him. He did not have to do all that work. The degree to which Posner's is a CIA book may be a question.

This fact is without question: At the very least, the CIA made Posner's book possible.

III

The "Enhancement" of Posner's Book

While there was good reason for it, we have neglected that pretty little girl too long. Let us now return to her and to Posner's affair with her, his absolute basis for his "closing the case" as he put it. Later will be time enough to report what he had in hand, and what was free to him that he could have copied and used from my files; information he knew about and did not want that came from and was about Nosenko and Oswald and what Nosenko said and what he knew.

Posner was either ignorant of the published Warren Commission testimony he boasted about having studied so diligently and even indexed himself, or worse, he did not dare use it. He would also have discovered as after more than twenty-five years I had forgotten: the Commission did not even keep the Willises' two daughters straight. They actually have testimony from Linda Kay instead of Rosemary.

For a man as vicious with words as Posner is, with the others writing in the field and with the Commission, it is not easy to believe that he would miss this opportunity to make himself look so much more important and so well informed with another of his usually politely phrased nasty comments. Only four pages after he gets into his key to his "closing" the case with the

Willis girl, he said—not for the first or the last time—what is quite true and is a lawyer's principle but what he did not practice with her and with quite a few others when he was not abiding by his own and oft-stated principle when it did not fit with his needs: *"Testimony closer to the event must be given greater weight than changes or additions made years later, when the witness's own memory is often muddied by television programs, films, books, and discussions with others."* (Page 235.)

Posner is a lawyer, a "Wall Street" lawyer at that. (He says it often enough, anyway.) He should have told his readers, most of whom lack knowledge of the law and do not know what testimony really is and what makes it a superior and more trustworthy source of information, that "Testimony" is what is sworn— under oath—and is therefore subject to prosecution if it is perjurious. It is given in a proceeding usually presided over by a judge. Testimony is also subject to confrontation and to refutation. Quoting what someone wrote about what someone else allegedly said is not nearly as probative. The person quoted may or may not have said what is quoted, or may or may not have known the truth. Either one could make mistakes or have a motive not to be truthful. And unless it is in an official proceeding, there are no penalties entailed for false representation. In addition, what Posner said earlier in his book about testimony applies here if it was "closer to the event (it) must be given greater weight." As most lawyers do when they are adversaries, Posner says what it suits his purpose to say one place, and pays no attention at all to his very own words in a different place when that suits his purposes.

Compare what he said with what he did in what we here address. Writing about those "new Zapruder enhancements" for which he needed a timing key, and writing without any source cited, making it a clear statement that he is writing about his own investigative derring-do, he wrote, as we have seen, that "beginning at frame 160, was a young girl in a red skirt and white top who was running along the left side of the President's car, down Elm Street, began turning to her right. But by frame 187, less than 1.5 seconds later, the enhancement clearly shows she had stopped, twisted completely away from the motorcade, and was staring back at the School Book Depository. That (little) girl was ten-year-old Rosemary Willis.''

It is here that he injected his diversion for which he used Moore, that his unnamed *"Some* believe the girl's reaction was because her father, Phil Willis, standing only ten feet away, told her to stop and come back toward him.'' At this point is his footnote 17, the one in which Posner attributes what he knew was not correct to "Interview with Jim Moore, March 9, 1993.''

What follows Posner's Moore diversion cannot be attributed to Moore as its source because it is text *following* his citation of Moore as his source in his footnote 17. If he sources what is next quoted, and nothing has been omitted in direct quotation of what Posner here wrote, it must be attributed to another source. What he says next is: "However, when Rosemary Willis was asked why she had stopped running with the President's car, she said, 'I stopped when I heard the shot.' '' Here he has source note 18. By this he attributes the girl's saying that the shot made her stop *and only that* to the source he cites in footnote 18. *His sole use of his source note 18 is to the Willis girl's reason for stopping.*

Then, referring to her stopping, he follows, nothing omitted in quotation, ''The Zapruder film is the visual confirmation that provides the timing.'' Posner has no indicated source for this. This, then, is his own personal and remarkable Perry Masonry; what he alleges *he* discovered *in the enhancement—and only in the enhancement.* This claim goes back to what Bob Loomis, Random House's executive editor and vice president told *Publishers Weekly*'s Robert Dahlin no later than April 1993, before the book's publication. In the issue dated May 3, Dahlin quotes Loomis as saying that Posner depended upon ''computer and laser enhancements of the eyewitness Zapruder film.''

Following what is quoted from Posner directly above, again nothing omitted in quotation, he again distracts and diverts with what is basically unnecessary in the book, but is absolutely essential to what our Supersherlock is up to when using source notes to pretend he is citing all the sources he uses so that he can claim the work of another as his own personal discovery: what is the very basis of this book. *And he cribbed it from a kid!*

He used tricky writing and tricky footnotes to hide it! We have seen what information is attributed to his source note 18. This is what he has directly following source 18: "The Zapruder film is the visual confirmation that provides the timing."

He has no source note here. He then says, nothing omitted: "In that split second, I thought it was a firecracker. But within maybe a tenth of a second, I knew it was a gunshot . . . I think I probably turned to look toward the noise, toward the Book Depository.' " And then his source note 19; his only source for what follows what he sourced in source note 18. This means that what is not in his footnote 19 source he represents himself as the source of. His footnote 19 is the only citing of his source for what he says after footnote 18. This includes that "The Zapruder film is the visual confirmation that provides the timing," the very basis of Posner's book.

Posner indicates no source other than himself for what he alone saw in that "enhanced film." He says that this is how *he* timed the first shot at Zapruder Frame 162. (He says that shot missed.)

He then refers to motions by the President and his wife to which he attributes his own interpretation and meaning to make them mean what they do not mean, that they are reacting to that missed, early shot at Frame 162. He then says that besides the girl and the first family, "Governor Connally's recollections and actions confirm a shot was fired before Frame 166." He cites no page numbers for that testimony.

There is no such "confirmation." There is no such testimony. Posner makes it up. When Connally testified in regard to frame numbers, he was firm in saying that he was shot later than Posner says he was, as in Volume IV, page 139.

Remember, Connally was alive long after Posner was down in Texas working on his book. Posner boasts of his 200 interviews. *He does not say he interviewed Connally.* Instead, he invents what he wants to have believed, and he attributes that to the now-deceased Connally.

After this tricky deal, Posner quotes Connally as saying he was looking over his right shoulder when he heard what he immediately identified as a rifle shot. Posner's citation of that testimony is to pages 132–3 earlier in the Connally testimony (in the Commissions Volume IV).

It is important to remember that in Posner's supposed establishing of the time of what he claims was the first shot, the shot he says missed, all he has attributed to anyone else is when the Willis girl stopped running.

Now for the truth.

Posner's source note 18 reads: "David Lui, 'The Little Girl Must Have Heard,' *The Dallas Times Herald,* June 3, 1979, H–3."

Before Posner started exploiting the JFK assassination, that newspaper went out of business. In the remote possibility anyone wanted to check Posner on that little girl hearing something, that newspaper library cannot be consulted. And how many people outside of Dallas have any reason to clip Dallas papers other than those Posner portrays as less than dependable sources?

And who ever heard of David Lui? He is not mentioned in any of the assassination books of which I know. But it happens I *do* remember David Lui.

Friends from New York to California sent me copies of that story from three other newspapers. It is not a *Dallas Times Herald* story. It was syndicated by *The Los Angeles Times.* A New Yorker sent me the story as it appeared in *The Washington Star* and *The San Francisco Chronicle.* They were not all used the same day. Some were shortened.

When Lui wrote his story in 1979 he was attending Brown University, in Providence, Rhode Island. When he was fifteen years old and a student in Beverly Hills (California) High School, he undertook an extra credit project on the JFK assassination. He had a bootleg copy of the Zapruder film. None of them was very clear. He also was able to buy a set of the Commission's twenty-six volumes. Here is how he began his story:

"I sat watching the silent Zapruder film for what must have been the 50th time that night. Suddenly, this time I saw something that startled me; a young girl running to keep pace with the presidential limousine stopped abruptly and turned toward the Texas School Book Depository—too early in the film, and before any shots were supposed to have been fired.''

In *The Boston Globe,* this story ran across the top of two pages, close to a full page in all. It is almost at the end that Lui reports he was later able to ask her about it that she told him she was running with the car and stopped when she heard a shot.

What this makes clear is that Posner attempted to cover his ''appropriation''—from a kid at that!—of what he attributed to his advanced computer enhancement that he says alone made it all possible! By crediting Lui only with the well-known fact that Rosemary had been running along the south side of Elm Street, he credited Lui with nothing else. He attributes Lui's ''discovery'' to himself through ''his'' computer enhancements!

What Posner actually claims it was not possible to observe until he got all that uncredited ''enhancement,'' this kid could and did see years earlier with his unaided eye and from a rather poor copy of the Zapruder film at that! He saw it and interviewed Rosemary about it; he reported it and by Posner's source note trickery Posner appropriated it.

This is how Posner became the darling of the major media and received all those high-flown credits from big name personalities who should have learned not to take a book by its author's or publisher's representation before vesting their reputations in unstinting praise of it. All those high-flown raves for what comes from a theft and a fake! A theft from a kid! And all that fakery of only this advanced ''enhancement'' making it all possible!

What is left? Only the theories Posner says he eschews and condemns in others!

What else he has on the assassination is nothing except more pseudo-science mumbo jumbo flimflammery, and it is not new in any event. What Posner wrote is not fact. It is what he wants to have believed is fact. His only allegedly factual basis was that ''enhancement.'' The only apparent enhancements were of Posner and of Random House. They had the TV networks fighting to get at what was only phony baloney and with the other attention they all had the country agog.

If this is not scandalous enough, there is more; more that makes "scandalous" into a praise, it is that bad.

Throughout, Posner brags up his personal diligent and conclusive scholarship. He is king of the heap and he knows it all. From his endless self-praise of his all-inclusive scholarship, it is obvious that he had to know about what he suppressed from his book and from his readers. There is no reason to limit this to suppressions by his omissions of what he had to know.

He actually claims to have read all of the Commission's twenty-six volumes, but in fact he had so little knowledge of them, he cites them as used by others and said of them other things that are not true. This, of course, raises questions all over again of where he got what he could not possibly have done for himself, how he could have read what exceeds the capability of the speediest of speed readers if he did nothing else in the time he had for his book, like traveling and conducting all those claimed 200 interviews. Two hundred in a year or so?

In fact he understated the number of words in those commission volumes by ten times. Yet at the same point he claims he read them.

Withal condemning those with whom he disagrees. He uses his assault on Sylvia Meagher, an assault that would have been hazardous were she still alive to respond, (articulate, eloquent, and passionate woman that she was) to boast about himself and the magnitude of the work he professes to have done alone and unassisted.

In the course of his attempted literary assassination of her on page 419, he is critical of her index, the only one available. In this he actually said that, ". . . the (Commission) volumes originally had only a name index. . . ." Glaringly false!

Only the testimony has an index, and it is a name index. But the even greater volume of pages in the appendix do not have even the "name" index this most preeminent of subject scholars says they have, and it is with them, and them alone, in his words, that the lack of any index other than Meagher's of course, makes it "almost impossible to work (in) effectively."

Where did that "originally" come from, preeminent scholar? They still have not been indexed by the government. It has made no index available.

The balance of his line partly quoted above on the difficulty of working in the Commission's volumes gives their word count as "more than 1 million words." Here he has a note on the bottom of the page to which we return.

The official estimate of the number of words in those volumes is not 1 million: it is 10 million.

What Posner deems not necessary to quote is what Meagher said in her index's explanatory note, her purpose, that she "hoped" her index "will enable scholars to test the assertions and conclusions in the Warren Report against their independent judgement...." The massive Warren Report is exhaustively noted to its claimed sources and it is written to convict Oswald. That, in Posner's concept of true scholarship, is fine. That it was careful not to cite and thus not to direct attention to what contradicted its conclusions or its interpretations of evidence, that also he regards as fine and scholarly. But for someone to provide a counterpart, access to other than what the Report says, that is simply terrible!

What makes Meagher "a committed leftist" is being accurate in saying in advance exactly what would be said of Oswald when he was arrested and when it was learned that he had a Russian wife. Posner makes it plain that any complaint about the politics of the writer being reflected in the book depends on the writer's politics. If it is loaded on the conservative side, with that view, as his book is, that is the way it should be. But if it is whatever he may mean by "her politics are clear throughout the book," her politics not being his politics, that is very, very wrong.

What are his political complaints against Meagher and her writing? Such things as (his words), "she charged that large numbers of the Dallas police force were members of right-wing extremist organizations...." (Page 419.) Is Posner on this planet or did he just get carried away with himself and the only true belief? It is beyond question that in what Meagher said about *some* of the Dallas police, she neither exaggerated nor erred, and it has for all these many years been anything but secret. And when it comes to Posner's complaint (all on the same page—419) that her "index reflects her bias that Oswald was innocent," how is that anymore biased than Posner's beginning with the assumption of Oswald's guilt? Or systematically pretending in his book that what tended to exculpate Oswald that Meagher did index does not exist? Enough illustrations (far from all, he provides that many), of his biases against Oswald and for the government and its official mythology will follow. There is, however, this difference: Posner's personal and professional honesty and integrity will be in question. In his complaints against Meagher, he makes it clear, anything and everything is right for him, the gander, but nothing the gander dislikes is good for the goose.

Posner's footnote condemning Meagher all over again, true gentleman that he is, says he read all those volumes, actually 10 million words, and he, in addition, indexed them because he found hers "biased." From the man who wrote *this* book, that is an appropriate criticism? His is openly biased in favor of the official "solution." So, "unable" to use hers, he "made a new card index." In addition to all he claims to have done *could he possibly have indexed 10 million words too?*

Her index, he pontificates, "reflects her bias that Oswald was innocent." Aside from his unhidden bias that Oswald was guilty, who needed more than the Commission's own citations, by volume and page number, in the back of its Report to find the allegedly incriminating evidence?

Or did he not read that Report either, but obtained what he used from it from another source?

Moreover, where does he get off complaining about the alleged bias of anyone else in an index when he uses his own "index" not only to reflect his political biases but even to argue!

With his claim that his book holds new biographical information about Oswald, does he index in it Oswald's politics, as important as they are? No. Does he have anywhere in his book index what Oswald said about the USSR, or about the American Communist Party? No. But he does have a listing under Oswald for "U.S., denounced by." He also, in this index, suggests what Oswald was not, with his listing of Oswald's alleged "anarchist behavior."

He did not have to do any research to learn about Oswald's politics because I published that in *Whitewash,* my first book, in which I do have a "politics" listing under Oswald, with many pages given. For example, on page 122: "Oswald's hatred of the Communist Party and the Soviet Union exude from 150 consecutive pages of his notes ... in Exhibit 97 of Volume 16, pages 283–84, he rages, 'The Communist Party of the United States has betrayed itself.' " Oswald also wrote that the U.S. Communist Party had betrayed the working class. The Soviet leaders he castigated as "fat, stinking politicians." These kinds of views expressed so extensively in such voluminous writings for a man so lacking in formal education are not worthy of indexing? It is, in fact, less than honest to refuse to index them.

If Posner had any interest at all in a scholarly study of Oswald's writings for his supposed definitive biography and had mentioned it to me, I would have directed him to a file drawer of copies of his writings which years ago I made duplicate copies of and filed all in one place for just such a scholarly interest, someone wanting to make an independent study of what Oswald wrote, not what hacks and hired pens said he wrote.

In Posner's claim to have read and indexed those massive twenty-six volumes of those 10 million words he also claims complete knowledge of the Commission's volumes. His book does not reflect this knowledge.

How, then, can this devotee of original sources explain his using (and using as his own work, no less,) Young Lui's story? How could he quote Lui's 1979 article, or that utterly meaningless note to the interview of Rosemary Willis by Marcia Smith-Durk, without reference to who she is, where it is or can be seen? And why did he cite nothing else?

That "a" Willis girl testified, and with all he said about the superiority of testimony closer to the time of the event, Posner does not mention. Her official testimony was before the Warren Commission. This is how Posner's book can be as "definitive"

as boasted: it finds the hearsay of a decade and a half later to be
so much superior to first-person, contemporaneous eyewitness
testimony that he makes no mention at all of what he says is
superior testimony closer to the event. Linda Kay Willis is the
then 15-year-old girl eyewitness who did testify (7H498–9). She
is a nonperson in Posner's definitive book so highly praised
because "it answers all questions."

Posner does prate, quoted above (from page 235) that testimony closer to the event must be given greater weight" because
with the passing of years recollections are influenced and
change. (Neither Lui's article or Smith-Durk's interview is
"testimony.")

Phil and Marilyn Willis had *two* daughters. Both were at the
scene of the crime with both parents, and both saw the impact
of bullets, as did their mother. As Phil, with whom I had a
friendly relationship and exchanged phone calls and letters told
me, Wesley Liebeler, the Commission's counsel who deposed
Linda Kay Willis, "called the wrong one."

It simply is not possible that this man who says he read and
indexed those volumes did not know of Linda Kay's sworn
testimony. His suppression of it—of its existence—magnifies
his other dishonesties and underscores his intent to be corrupt
and try to corrupt our officially corrupted history even more.

In response to Liebeler's asking Linda Kay Willis if she
heard what she took to be shots, she *testified, under oath:* "Yes.
I heard one. Then there was a little bit of time, and then there
were two real fast bullets together. When the first one hit, well,
the President turned from waving to the people, and he grabbed
his throat, and he kind of slumped forward, and then . . ." —and
this requires close attention—". . . I couldn't tell where the
second shot went."

*She said it was the second shot that missed, and she was
looking and listening!*

If Posner had not suppressed this he would have had no book
at all! Where was she, Linda Kay, when she saw the impact
on the President? *"I was right in line with the sign (Stemmons
Freeway) and the car and I wasn't very far away, but I couldn't
tell where the shot came from."*

Like Rosemary, she also "followed along the street with the car."

Sure you didn't see Linda Kay "enhanced," too, Gerald Posner?

She testified that she "saw the President get hit in the head," too. "Actually?" Liebeler asked and she again said, "Yes." Liebeler translated her estimated distance from the President to be about 20 feet. That was close.

Liebeler kept Linda Kay's testimony brief. He could have asked her more questions about the shooting and how she saw the victims react, for example. But neither he nor Posner wanted that.

Like Liebeler, Posner could have spoken to Mrs. Marilyn Willis. She was right there, near her girls, also looking at the President when the shots hit him. Would not one ordinarily believe that an older and more experienced person would be a better witness than a child? (Unless, of course, the child is "enhanceable.")

From what Phil Willis told me, and I have it in a memo, the testimony on the shooting that his wife and older daughter would have given was that the President's fatal wound was from the front.

The testimony of either would have presented an impossible situation to the Commission as it would have to Posner, to both for the same reason. It should, if not ignored, have made impossible the lone-assassin preconception of the Warren Commission and of Posner's preconceived "smash" book that so "definitively" and all those other many encomiums says: There was only the one assassin: Oswald.

Oswald could not simultaneously have shot from both sides.

(For those who doubt there was this official preconception of a lone assassin, proof of it is throughout my published work. I cite in particular the Introduction to *Post Mortem,* "Conclusions First." Being prepared for publication as I write this is unquestionable official documentation of it in *Never Again!* That book begins with this official documentation from the highest of places in the government.)

When Liebeler repeated the same questions she gave the

same responses, repeating that it was the second shot she heard that she did not see impact, *not* the one Posner says missed.

If Posner read and indexed those volumes as he says he did, he would obviously have known of Linda Kay's testimony, and in knowing about it, he also knew that it refutes his concoction of a new semi-official mythology, and that explains why he makes no mention of her sworn testimony.

Need anything more be said of Posner and his book than he says for himself in the foregoing?

Need anything more be said about the publisher not having the traditional—nonfiction peer review? There could not have been an authentic one without my knowledge.

Did Posner and his publisher impose upon the trust of all of those who wrote those glowing dust-jacket endorsements? Those who plugged the book with major TV attention, major reviews, glowing news stories?

Is there anyone whose trust was not imposed upon?

Computer enhancements, huh? Isn't that how Stephen Spielberg brought dinosaurs back?

IV
Posner Suppresses What the CIA Disclosed. Why?

Posner makes a big deal of his interview of Nosenko. He does not tell the reader that the CIA delivered Nosenko to him, naturally. But he pretends that in his interview he learned from Nosenko what was not already public knowledge. From what is in Posner's book, he learned nothing at all. There is nothing of any importance he reports getting from Nosenko. Posner used that interview for nothing more than sucker-bait promotional material for his book. Those not familiar with the available fact, particularly overly busy people like those big-name types who provided prepublication promotional statements, have no way of knowing these things. Posner and Random House suckered them in particular with the pretense that Posner got what is new and important from Nosenko.

What Posner does not report but what is important he did not have to get from Nosenko because I published it in 1975 in *Post Mortem,* a book Posner supposedly read.

What I say there is considerably abbreviated, but I also stated that in addition to what I was then publishing from previously secret government records, "I have obtained hundreds of relevant pages, seek more and will be writing about this separately." (Page 627.)

Posner never asked me for any of that information or for copies of any of those many documents.

With all those once-withheld records, some classified Top Secret, I should explain why I then devoted so little space to Nosenko and the information he had and gave the FBI. (Pages 627–9.)

After my first book was rejected by more than a hundred publishers internationally, I decided to publish it myself. I became and remain, I suppose, the country's smallest publisher. My wife and I did all the work other than the actual printing. She substituted for the printing typesetter and I, having been taught by my friend, the late Sammie Abbott how to do it, did the makeup. Sammie did the covers.

Books are printed in what are termed "signatures," often of thirty-two pages or of sixteen, depending on the printing presses used. When I made *Post Mortem* up for printing there were four pages that would have been blank. So I used them for Nosenko information. Although the Nosenko content has no relationship to the rest of the book, wanting that information and knowledge of its availability to be disseminated, even for the kissers of official ass like Posner as well as for those with a genuine interest in trying to establish what truth could be established, I filled every available line in those four pages with information. It was considerably condensed, but it did identify the documents I used, held the essence and was a record for the future.

If Posner had not been playing Dr. Faustus to the CIA as Mephistopheles, he would have paid closer attention to how I began that much condensed writing:

"Coming exposés will prove the CIA withheld vast amounts of relevant data from the Commission and that the Commission knew it, knew the CIA would and did lie, and allowed the CIA to suppress those records which would embarrass it. (Instead of investigating the crime, the CIA investigated critics of the covering up. I have copies of some of its espionage on me.)"

If Posner were what he is not, a traditional American writer caring about his country and its future and holding to traditional American beliefs, learning—if he did not already know it—that the CIA, for which it is prohibited by law—"instead of investigating the crime . . . investigating critics of the cover-up. I have copies of some of its espionage on me"—would at the least have been offended. Anyone should be outraged by such anti-American, authoritarian behavior by the intelligence agencies. They were not to spy on or intrude into the lives of Americans.

Posner and his wife Trisha were here. Trisha's receipt for the number of pages of my records she copied says they got 724 copies on February 13, 14, and 15, 1992. They also borrowed and returned some photographs. As Gerald noted in his acknowledgments I "allowed him full run of my basement, filled with file cabinets . . ." (Page 504.) He also noted that I granted access to those hundreds of thousands of previously withheld official records to all writing in the field. He did not report that in fact I do not and cannot supervise those uses of my records and I also allowed all to use our copier.

He makes no reference to his getting free access to copies of those records I got only after years of the most difficult and costly lawsuits under the Freedom of Information Act. This omission is explained by a careful reading of his notes. In them he pretends he got those records by his own work. As a result, for all his self-described herculean effort and all the knowledge he wants the reader to believe he has, he cannot even explain and he does not explain the meanings of the file numbers or why on some there is no file identification. In at least one instance that I notice without looking for them, he is so ignorant of the FBI's main assassination file number at its Dallas office he misread the poor copy I got from the FBI and gave his readers an impossible number for those desiring to check him out or to learn more.

At the time of that writing I did have "hundreds of relevant pages" and it is true that "coming exposés will prove the CIA withheld vast amounts of relevant data . . ."

It is particularly true of what Posner says about Nosenko and the CIA and about what he says about the shooting. I filed two of that dozen FOIA lawsuits against the FBI for the results of its scientific testing, including all the evidence relating to the shooting. It was over the first of those two cases that the Congress amended the investigatory files exemption of the Act in 1974 to make FBI, CIA, and similar files accessible under the provision of FOIA. If Posner had been truthful I would have given him pictures that prove some of what he would be writing, the writing about which he deceived me. But, obviously, Posner did not want that. If he had been interested in the second of those two lawsuits for the results of secret scientific testing he would have found the suppressed scientific proof that Oswald did not fire a rifle that terrible day. But, again, Posner did not want that. Dr. Faustus wanted to have and to enjoy his Mephistopheles time.

That was a remarkably accurate forecast. In addition to the file drawer of previously secret Nosenko records I had obtained by the time the Posners were here, a relatively large number of pages were released toward the end of 1993. That were pursuant to an act of Congress requiring disclosure of all JFK assassination information that was not exempt from disclosure by law. In 1993 a reported million pages from the records of all agencies became available at the Archives. In testifying that November to what he had learned from his examination of those disclosed by the CIA, University of Maryland professor, John N. Newman, then with eighteen years in Army Intelligence said, "A great deal more is at stake than who killed President Kennedy. What is at stake is nothing less than the faith of the people in our institutions."

Newman is the author of the widely and justifiedly acclaimed *JFK and Viet Nam,* (New York, Warner Books, 1992). In devoting almost a full newspaper page to Newman and his testimony *The Washington Post* of November 18, 1993, asked in its main headline, "Did Democracy Die In Dallas?" The subhead is, "John Newman says the government's lies about the JFK assassination are tearing America apart."

Posner et al contribute mightily to the continued tearing apart of the country so clearly and extensively reflected in the many thousands of letters and phone calls I got and continue to get from strangers, many of whom are young. A not inconsiderable proportion of these letters are from those not born at the time of the assassination and they are terribly, terribly disturbed by the unacceptable claimed official solution of it.

The *Post*'s Jefferson Morley reported that John Conyers, veteran Democratic congressman from Michigan, was visibly troubled by Newman's testimony before his Government Operations Committee of the House of Representatives.

I believe that by the time Newman, whose experience in Army Intelligence prepares him so admirably well to examine those newly disclosed records, has finished his work, an entirely different picture of Oswald will emerge, as well as the extent of the lied-about CIA interest in him of which Newman has informed me.

Some of this I reported from what Nosenko told the FBI that Posner had no interest in.

After I published *Post Mortem* in 1975, I was then not able to do further writing or to "expose" that "the CIA withheld vast amounts more" information because as soon as I had the book in the hands of the printer I was virtually immobilized and then hospitalized for acute thrombophlebitis, a circulatory disorder that can cause excruciating pain.

Knowing I had all those records and made them available without any supervision at all Posner did not ask me a single question about them. Not even how to find them more rapidly than an uninformed search could take.

They do hold what exposes one of his many ugly little services to the CIA in his book.

I was not in a position to volunteer where he would find these and related records because I assumed he was an honest writer, writing an honest book. I did not know the kind of book he was writing. But he deceived me about what he was writing. He told me he was writing a book limited to exposing commercialization and exploitation of the assassination by some of that motley crew generally known as "critics" and on all deception of the people about that tragedy. I am all for setting that record straight.

If Posner had not lied to me about the book he was writing, if he had told me of any interest in Nosenko, I would have told him of my file drawer of Nosenko records. From the book he published, however, it is clear that he had no interest in the truth and would have had no interest in that considerable volume of Nosenko records.

The thrombophlebitis with which I began a decade and a half of the most intensive FOIA litigation in a dozen of those suits that filled my basement with filing cabinets was followed by a number of surgeries. Post-surgical complications when I was already a septuagenarian imposed serious limitations on what I am able to do. The use of the basement stairs is difficult, excessively tiring and not without potential hazard for me. So I led Posner and his wife to the basement and showed them how the files are arranged. I showed them where each kind is located, especially those in which he had explained his representedly exclusive interest. If he had been truthful in describing his book, he would have been able to read and copy hundreds of pages that would have made his book impossible for an honest writer. This is true of all parts of his book other than its section on Jack Ruby, the man who killed Oswald.

In what I quote above from the beginning of those rushed and bobtailed Nosenko pages in *Post Mortem* I refer to the "vast amounts of relevant data withheld" by the CIA. Is it not at this point, worth considering whether there is or can be any connection between Random House's rushing of Posner's book into sales and promotions ahead of the announced schedule, even at the risk of losing some reviews thereby, to coincide with the actual flooding of that ocean of records into public availability? The book did reap a rich harvest of free and major publicity from the washoff of the great attention to the making of those records available, if "available" is the reality.

(Parenthetically, I note what escaped all media comment at that time; that the mere volume of those records can defy access. There were 1,000,000 pages in most accounts, and that is a volume no individual and no major media component could begin to cope with. The minimum cost of copies would be a quarter of a million dollars. It would also require at least 150 file cabinets. Who has this kind of money to invest in those papers and who has the space or would rent or construct the space for storing them and for getting access to them? As with all earlier disclosures of JFK assassination records, the government made a media event of it. The media were hot for it the first day and by the third day it was no longer interested.)

With all the Nosenko information I had free for his taking, Posner had no interest at all. Again, if he were an honest American writer who believed in the fine tradition of American writers going back to Zenger, who established basic rights for those who followed him or who believed in the responsibilities imposed upon us by our founding fathers, he should have been interested in a sentence on the next page of *Post Mortem*: "Nosenko told the CIA (not one report from which can be found in the Commission's files), and the FBI and the Russians actually believed Oswald was a "sleeper" or "dormant" American agent." This was the first reason for the KGB's keeping Oswald under the surveillance Posner does not report. (Such agents are also called "agent in place," as for future use.) Posner also had no interest in that. Not while he was here, nor after he left, not in our phone conversations or letters—absolutely no interest. Period!

Two paragraphs later I wrote that, "The CIA could not deny the FBI access to Nosenko" (referring to when he first defected). FBI agents known to have interviewed him are Maurice A. Taylor, Donald R. Walter, and Alekso Popanovich, beginning February 26, 1964. This is a date that would have galvanized an honest, impartial writer seeking truth to take to the people or a nation that, if its democratic system functions, requires truth and knowledge. We return to this.

Although Posner should have known it, I quoted from one of the Commission's executive sessions that dealt specifically and in general with Oswald as an agent. Those sessions were so secret, classified "Top Secret," the Commission's staff was barred from them: "The CIA knew, Dulles told the Commission, the FBI had no agents in Russia." My citation is to the stenographic transcript of the session of January 27, 1964. After I obtained it in FOIA litigation, I published it in facsimile in *Whitewash IV,* along with other relevant documents. Posner got it from me. He had it. He knew.

So, Posner did not care about the Russian belief that Oswald could be an American agent, or that I had all those records he could have, or that if he had been an American agent, Oswald could have not have been from the FBI. What, then, did Posner really ask about? Did Posner go into the possibility that Oswald might have been an American agent with Nosenko? What, then did Posner write? Not a damned thing that meant anything does he reflect getting from Nosenko, whom the CIA made available to him, an extreme rarity, as Posner is not reluctant to boast about.

Did the CIA impose any ground rules, any restrictions on Posner's interview of Nosenko? Were there any restrictions, any taboos? Posner makes no mention of any restrictions, if the CIA imposed any. But then it had no need to do that because Posner did it for the CIA, as his book makes clear.

Pretending the honesty he lacks, pretending the impartiality that is foreign to him, pretending not to be snuggled in the CIA's bed, he misleads the reader into believing that he also tells the whole story of how the CIA abused Nosenko, and why.

It should by now be no surprise that he does no such thing! And never intended to!

What Posner does report about this he presents as the result of his own work. That is false. Worse, he hides the secret from his readers and from those who in the future may have an interest in this sordid incident in our history and who make the mistake of trusting Posner and his book.

With the extraordinary attention Random House, aided by the CIA, got for Posner's book, many traces searchers of the future will find that lead to Posner's book will be impossible to miss. They will thus be guided to a work of the most thoroughgoing, intended, professional dishonesty—and that in a field that suffers no lack of them.

I do not use these words lightly. Before I stopped annotating

Posner's book to do this writing, I found such a number of the most deliberate dishonesties I fear no challenge from him or from Random House. Were they to do that, there would then be a public record of what without that will exist only in private, for scholars of the future. I cannot use all of them in this book, there are that many.

It should be no surprise that of all I can remember without searching my files—and they are on paper but I have no need to search for them—all have the same intent: covering up for the official miscreants, for the CIA and for the official mythology misrepresented as a "solution" to that most terrible of crimes.

In his apologist's role, Posner adopts the new math of the unofficial apologists that traces back to the misbegotten miserable mess made by the House Select Committee on Assassination, the strange but major-media accepted notion that the Commission could have been wrong in just about everything it did and by some mystery or magic was right in its conclusions nonetheless. The apologists always have some such convenient self-deception they—thanks to the major media—always got away with. Such as when it was proven that the world's best shots could not duplicate the shooting attributed to Oswald they said that Oswald just got lucky that one time. This is an area of one of Posner's most blatant dishonesties, where he says Oswald was a superb marksman, when the Marines officially evaluated him as a "rather poor shot." No wonder! On his last testing Oswald scored one point over the minimum score required of all in the military, and he was then aided in passing only by his fellow Marines who scored misses as well as hits as the testimony of former Marine Nelson Delgado makes laughingly clear. (8H228ff; *Oswald in New Orleans,* pages 92, 94–101, 107.)

An uninformed person reading Posner on the impediments to Nosenko's defection and on his subsequent longlasting, incredible, subhuman mistreatment by the CIA for close to three years would get the impression that Posner really exposed that fully. He alone, as usual, too. As usual, he again misrepresents. Cleverly, lawyerlike. In fact, he covered that up too! And worst of all, going back to that KGB suspicion that Oswald could have been an American agent, he not only suppressed this, he fails to report its significance in what happened to Nosenko after he reported it, such really terrible abuse he is lucky to have survived it, literally and emotionally.

Posner's Nosenko chapter, his third, is titled "The War of the Defectors." It has ninety-nine numbered notes. Of those, more than half are citations to Posner's interview of Nosenko. It has one citation to the House Select Committee on Assassination hearing which is not to the CIA's formal testimony relating to Nosenko, and one to that committee's report. The reader is thus given to believe that all the information in the chapter is new and that Posner personally developed it when he interviewed Nosenko. This is also how Posner makes his contribution to the historical record appear to be. This is false. The Posner version is ever so much kinder to the CIA than the CIA's own official admission of the beyond-belief evils it inflicted on the man. Posner also names an entirely different person in the Department of Justice as responsible there than the CIA did *officially.*

Readers should remember Posner's criticism of Sylvia Meagher for her alleged political beliefs allegedly biasing her book and her index.

After a fantasy beginning to this chapter in which he palms off the CIA's nonsensical reason for not trusting Nosenko, Posner starts to tell his version on page 36. Posner there says that Nosenko sought to defect in Switzerland in January 1964.

What Posner does not say here is that a year earlier Nosenko had done the same thing at the same place. That gave the CIA more time than it needed to check on Nosenko, as it then should have and probably did before January 1964.

Posner says that the CIA "dispatched 37-year-old Tennent 'Pete' Bagley and an agent fluent in Russian, George Kisevalter, to meet Nosenko four times in a safe house near Geneva's center." Those meetings, Posner says, were taped, and the tapes were transcribed. Posner admits that the information Nosenko provided was good information. Instead of citing the CIA's public evaluation, Posner, still pretending that there was no such

thing, cites another book; one by Tom Mangold, a British reporter and another Faust. His book was largely based on information provided by the CIA in return for his protecting the CIA
as an institution in that book, *Cold Warrior*. He blamed all its
excesses on the then dead and buried James Jesus Angleton,
who had headed CIA counterintelligence. (New York, Simon &
Schuster, 1991.)

Posner then says that while Bagley was "ecstatic" over what
Nosenko disclosed, his state of ecstacy ended when he returned
to Washington. Angleton, dead when Posner wrote his book,
remember, "was convinced no matter what Nosenko said that
he was a KGB plant." Angleton turned Bagley around, and
thus it is that in Posner's version once again the CIA as an
institution is exculpated as were those others involved who out-
lived the well-known super-paranoid Angleton, even though the
names of some are public.

A rather thick file of CIA records I did not get from the CIA,
contemporaneous records, give an entirely different account of
what really happened in Geneva, not after Bagley and Kisevalter
returned to Washington. Those records, which it now is obvious
Posner would have shunned like cholera, make it without question that almost beginning the moment Nosenko turned up,
someone in the Geneva station started trying to persuade
headquarters that Nosenko was a "plant" and should not be
allowed to defect. The reasons given were so childish in their
transparent falseness that they had to be replaced with new
reasons no less senseless when they collapsed on superficial
examination. This was the immediate CIA Geneva behavior,
not only after the team returned to Washington or CIA headquarters. Nosenko then had to lie to force the issue and he
was allowed to defect.

Not by accident Posner says (page 39) that on arrival in
Washington, Nosenko "was placed in a nice comfortable safe
house." On the same page Posner then skips from February to
June 24, when Richard Helms, soon to be the CIA's director
and then deputy head of its dirty-work department with the
euphemistic title of "Plans," told Warren Commission chairman Earl Warren that the CIA "doubted Nosenko's credibil-

ity.'' In fact, Helms and others from the CIA threatened the Commission so it would not interview Nosenko. Posner then writes—still on that one page, so much did Posner condense it, that "Helms did not tell the Chief Justice that since early April, with the backing of Attorney General Robert Kennedy, Nosenko had been under hostile interrogation."

To refer to that as merely "hostile" and as "interrogation" only is to praise it. Those with good memories that can carry them back to September 15, 1978, and were looking at TV or listening to the radio broadcasts of the CIA's official testimony to the House of Representatives on that barbarity may recall the unprecedented truth.

The truth and the fact that Posner here pretends did not exist. To puff himself and his case "closing" up he makes not a single mention of the fact that *most of the information he attributes to his private, secret interview of Nosenko* and even much more significant information was broadcast coast to coast when the CIA gave its testimony to that House committee.

The CIA called a former officer, not a spook, back from retirement to make a close and independent study of all its Nosenko records and then to testify to their content, *for the CIA,* as its official witness and confessor.

That CIA witness was John Hart. He testified that September 15th day. His testimony is published in the committee's second volume of JFK assassination hearings beginning on page 487. Posner makes not a single reference to this or even to Hart's name, as his index (page 593) reflects. His readers do not learn from him that it existed. This apotheosis of blatant dishonesty led the uninformed to believe it did not exist.

In Hart's *official* testimony—remember Posner's cracks about Sylvia Meagher for her supposed political bias?—the CIA identified the Department of Justice official with whom from the first and throughout the CIA conferred as Deputy Attorney General Nicholas Katzenbach. *Not as Robert Kennedy (as Posner says twice on page 79)!*

So much for Posner's political neutrality and his criticism of others for the beliefs he attributes to them.

If this is not enough to "open the case" on Posner, more

follows. If that is not enough, let us go to why Posner recounted the early stages of Nosenko's defection other than as the CIA's own records record it, with the most vigorous CIA opposition to his defection virtually immediately in Geneva.

In Posner's account, nothing happened between the time Nosenko was nested in that nice and comfortable house in one of the better sections of northwest Washington, the "Embassy Row" area, and the date he does not give for when, in "early April" that "hostile interrogation" began.

While the disclosed CIA records I got from the FBI, not from the CIA, which steadfastly refused to live within the law of the land, contain the cockamamie excuses cooked up to prevent Nosenko's defection, there is no indication in them of the more likely real reason: the CIA knew very well what Nosenko's official responsibilities in the KGB were. It therefore had every reason to believe that as soon as Oswald was arrested the man in the KGB who would have handled all it had on Oswald was Yuri Nosenko!

Nosenko knew all the KGB knew or suspected about Oswald.

Predictably, that is precisely what happened, as those FBI records disclosed to me state.

With this in mind, Payback Posner's account is worth emphasis, so I repeat it: In his account, nothing happened between the time Nosenko nested down in that nice comfortable house, and the date Posner here does not give—"early April" for when that "hostile interrogation" began.

But something *did* happen. Posner's omission of it seems to be deliberate. He got the information from me in February 1992 when he and his wife visited us. It is in *Post Mortem* on the pages quoted above. If, for any reason, Posner preferred not to cite my book, it even gives the numbers of the Commission's records I used in what I wrote. CDs (for Commission Documents) 434 and 451. Those are the FBI reports on its interviews with Nosenko. Nosenko, telling the FBI that Oswald had an openly anti-USSR record within the USSR also told them, as I reported where cited above, that the KGB suspected that "Oswald was a 'sleeper' or 'dormant American agent.'" (They are also referred to as "agents in place".)

It was on February 4, 1964, that Nosenko defected and it was on February 26 that the FBI interviewed him and he told it of the KGB's suspicion that Oswald was an American agent. (*Post Mortem,* page 627.)

The CIA did not have to be told, as its former director, Allen Dulles, told his fellow Warren Commissioners, that the FBI had no agents in Russia. (*Post Mortem,* page 628.) But if, for some reason not apparent, Posner had to be told, he had it in *Post Mortem* and he also had it in the facsimile reproduction of that January 27, 1964, top secret commission executive session transcript in *Whitewash IV.*

Those who believe that what the CIA says can always be depended upon should read that lengthy transcript beginning on page 48. By the time they reach page 62 they may be prepared for former CIA Director Allen Dulles, when he, along with the other Commissioners expecting perpetual secrecy, told them that swearing falsely under oath, the felony of perjury, is right and proper and is sometimes required. He also said that he might not have told the secretary of defense the truth.

So, in the unclosed case against Posner, he suppressed these significant facts and misrepresented others that are known to indulge his own politics.

Aside from protecting the CIA in it all, he omitted what my files—to which he had access—also show: that the FBI immediately hand-delivered to the CIA its reports on its interview with Nosenko. That informed the CIA that Nosenko said that the KGB suspected Oswald was an American agent. That could not have meant for the FBI because it had no agents there.

It fingered the CIA!

And it was as soon as the CIA learned from the FBI that Nosenko could have pointed a finger at it that his treatment by the CIA changed abruptly from princely to subhuman barbarism. It was that for almost three years! Inconceivable torture all that time, all that time in isolation for the arcane tortures the CIA dreamed up for him and to which Hart testified. In isolation, without so much as a window, plus those terrible acts by the CIA. Not by Angleton, as Posner would place the blame. It was the CIA as an institution.

The Posner case is not yet closed. Far from it.

Beyond belief as it is that any American writer could bring himself to write such a knowingly false, distorted and dishonest account of one of the most awful things any part of our government has ever done to any human being would rewrite our history to protect the CIA or could bring himself to do such totally anti-American things for the book the CIA gave him with or without other rewards, Posner did more.

On page 39 he gets around to dating this change in Nosenko's treatment by the CIA. It was on April 4. He begins his account by saying that "Nosenko's ordeal had started on April 4, 1964, when he was driven to a three-story safe house in a Washington suburb. Later he mentions that in that nice place Nosenko was confined to and isolated in its attic.

It took the CIA fourteen months to build the brick tank in which Nosenko then was confined at Camp Peary, Virginia, without windows or anything else, even something to read, and with inadequate food from which he then suffered as he did from the lack of toothpaste and any care at all. While Posner makes it clear that Nosenko was treated badly, his account portrays it as far less abusive than that testified to and acknowledged officially for it by the CIA official witness, John Hart. As Posner eases his way to the end he admits that it was not easy for Nosenko to "keep his sanity" but he continues to limit the blame for it all to "Angleton and Bagley." (Page 41.) The worst that Posner attributes to that pair alone, saying they "debated drugging him to hasten his breakdown . . . an assortment of drugs were considered, including a so-called truth serum, an amphetamine, and even LSD." (Pages 41–42.) That was far, very far from all, as Hart did testify. He testified to a deliberate attempt to drive Nosenko crazy so he could be confined and stifled in an institution, to various tortures and even ways of killing him. One was to fly him out over the ocean and then drop him into it.

Endless, endless, awful, subhuman torture for all that time, and then the American government intelligence officers plotted murder!

This was the CIA! Posner knew it. And he not only does not say it, he softens that unprecedented, official CIA abuse of a human being justified only by the fantasies imagined by the sick of mind in high position in the CIA and tolerated in silence by all there who knew of it.

The pretended justifications of this were themselves insane. How anyone in the CIA, which is supposedly composed of intelligent, well educated, sophisticated, politically informed and mature people—analysts on whom the safety of the country depends—could have believed any of it is incomprehensible.

Some analysts! Can anyone without his doctor of philosophy degree believe for a minute that the USSR or its KGB preferred the hawk Johnson to the dove Kennedy?

The assassination made that change automatic.

Posner even suppresses what was probably the most public, the most sensational, the most stunning and politically significant disclosure of any KGB spying ever when Ambassador Adlai Stevenson rose and addressed the Security Council of the United Nations with eloquence and passion. He was seen and heard throughout the world and reported by the press of the world. He held in his hand and displayed prominently a beautifully sculptured large seal of the United States, a ''gift'' to our Moscow embassy by the USSR. Without mention of Nosenko's name, Stevenson then shocked the Security Council, if not much of the world, by declaring that a microphone had been hidden in that ''gift'' and that it transmitted every word spoken in the ambassador's office.

Hart testified that this information and the discovery of many other bugs in that embassy is only part of what came from Nosenko.

With a minor attribution to Mangold, Posner again pretends that all that is known he got from Nosenko, even when he was reporting ever so much less than the CIA admitted publicly it had learned from him.

That is not all. Posner had to have known of two earlier interviews Nosenko (meaning the CIA), gave during the chilliest time of the cold war. The first was to the politically acceptable Washington editor of the politically acceptable *Readers Digest,* John Barron. In his much earlier book, *KGB,* Barron disclosed some of the valuable intelligence Nosenko gave the CIA. His book even identified spies Nosenko exposed by name.

No. Barron is not in Posner's bibliography (page 579).

V

How Posner "Found" That the Commission Was Right After All

What made me think that there was something familiar about what Posner presented as his own work with all that modern superscience did come to mind when some time after its September 5, 1993, publication date I was sent a copy of the lead *Case Closed* book review in *The San Francisco Chronicle*. It was by Patricia Holt, the *Chronicle*'s book editor and it did not go into panegyrics of praise. At the end of her lengthy and perceptive review she quotes Posner as quoting William Manchester, father of the JFK administration "Camelot" nonsense as saying "there is no evidence whatever that there was one," referring to a conspiracy. Her concluding paragraph is, "You can't say that by Posner's account, surely. In fact, the only reason "Case Closed" works as a title is that readers may be so sick of JFK assassination books they couldn't possibly stomach another one."

This, however, is not what triggered my recollection.

In her "Between the Lines" column on the second page she says what she did not say in her review. It is not lengthy and it deserves quotation in full:

Assassination Enigma Endures

That was quite an ad from Random House in a recent issue of *The New York Times* for Gerald Posner's *Case Closed* (see review on cover). Above mug shots and selected quotations (Jim Garrison: ''The JFK assassination was a homosexual thrill-killing'') by five authors and a film maker (Oliver Stone), the headline announced, ''GUILTY/Of Misleading the American Public.'' The ad smacks of playing dirty and sounds a little lame. If Posner's book should be judged on its own merits, why stoop to the ''Most-Wanted'' poster approach?

Of course, using selective information to prove one's case is common practice among JFK assassination authors. But Posner wants to distance himself from all others; he wants his book to be regarded as so fair and complete that after reading it, we'll say, OK, that's the end of it— ''case closed.''

But take the case of Failure Analysis Associates, the Menlo Park firm that used computer enhancements to reconstruct the JFK assassination for a 1992 study. Posner refers to that study repeatedly but does not explain that Failure Analysis was commissioned by the American Bar Association to create its reconstruction for the ABA's mock trial of Lee Harvey Oswald in San Francisco last year. The trial ended with a hung jury.

According to Angela Meyer of Failure Analysis, ''Our job for the ABA was to provide evidence and expert witnesses for *both* the defense and the prosecution.'' Posner appears to draw from testimony for the prosecution's case, not the defense's case.

Although Failure Analysis was not asked to provide its own opinion of Oswald's guilt or innocence, the company's CEO, Roger McCarthy (who testified for the defense at the mock trial), offered what host Brian Banmiller called ''a startling conclusion'' during the TV program ''On the Money'' on July 31.

Failure Analysis, announced Banmiller, ''made a compelling argument that Lee Harvey Oswald did not act alone." According to McCarthy, the gunman "gave up some awfully good shots to take some awfully bad shots" to "(drive) the quarry into a second shooting" by other assassins.

Banmiller then remarked, "Few sharpshooters, much less Oswald, could hit a moving target taking shots as rapidly as Oswald supposedly did." He asked McCarthy, "Can it be done?" McCarthy responded, "I can't. I'm the best shot I know. I can't do that."

Banmiller concluded, "Thirty years later, no one, not even Failure Analysis, is ready to say conclusively who killed President Kennedy." Case open—

Then I remember that fat file I have on that ABA mock trial, but not one of those many news accounts mentions Failure Analysis. I probably forgot all about that ABA mock trial of Oswald because at that time I was working concentratedly on *Never Again!*

So, with McCarthy's name, I wrote him on September 17. When I received no answer I wrote him again, telling him that I would much prefer not to but if I did not hear from him I would have to report that when I asked him for whatever information he could provide he did not respond. Then I did get an informative letter from Dr. Angela Meyer, Failure Analysis's Manager of Client Services and a participant in the work done for the American Bar Association. Because her letter is neutral, really impartial and much calmer than under the same circumstances I would have written I wrote immediately and asked for her permission to use it. Except for the last paragraph, in which she wishes me well with this book and looks forward to reading it, her letter, in full and unchanged follows:

Dear Mr. Weisberg:

Thank you very much for your letters dated September 17th and September 29th. As we received both letters within the last two days, any delay in our response has been a function of the Post Office.

I am familiar with your work having read your books last year during our trial preparing for the American Bar Association (ABA) Section of Litigation's Mock Trial, "U.S. vs. Oswald." In fact, your work resides in our in-house library. With your permission, I would like to spend the next portion of this letter describing to you the background of our work for the ABA Mock Trial so that you are more familiar with why we created these animations and why they are being utilized so much now, in the 30th anniversary year of the JFK assassination.

Background to the Investigation

Failure Analysis Associates, Inc. (FaAA) is the nation's leading consulting firm dedicated to the investigation, analysis, and prevention of failures of an engineering or scientific nature. Our work is well-known throughout the litigation field and we pride ourselves in utilizing the most state-of-the-art techniques in engineering analysis and demonstrative evidence preparation. This is why we were contacted by the ABA.

In March, 1992, members of the Litigation Section of the ABA approached FaAA to assist with a Mock Trial presentation for their 1992 Annual Meeting in San Francisco later that year. The ABA asked FaAA to provide expert witness testimony for both sides of the litigation—a first for our organization. We were also asked to provide all demonstrative evidence (courtboards, video, graphics, and computer animation). After much discussion, the decision was made to put Lee Harvey Oswald on "trial" at the event. Please be advised that this was a Mock Trial designed to *educate* attorneys on proper trial techniques as well as the use of technology to display demonstrative evidence. This trial was not used as a forum to prove or disprove that Oswald killed President Kennedy.

Trial Preparation

It was determined that the Prosecution would consider the following issues: The Magic or Tumbling Bullet Theory, Injury Analysis, and Path Trajectory of the Bullets. The Defense team, of which I was a member, concerned itself with Ballistics, Other Potential Firing Positions/Assassins, as well as "shooting holes" in the Prosecution's case. Both sides utilized the following background information: Warren Commission Report, House Select Committee Report, "Crossfire" as well as a copy of the Zapruder film. In addition, either side could acquire additional materials if necessary, if approved by the other side. That is how we acquired your books. Latimer's medical work was also used extensively and we had many discussions with Larry Howard in Dallas as well.

The Prosecution

The work that the Prosecution team presented you have seen in Posner's book. The lead member of the team was Dr. Robert Piziali, a V.P. and Manager of our Biomechanics Group. Injury analysis was performed using information provided in the record as well as photographs that have appeared in numerous books and articles. The Zapruder film was enhanced and each frame captured as a still to analyze the movements of the vehicle's occupants. During this analysis, the Prosecution was able to detect movement in the lapel flap on Governor Connally's jacket which prompted them to associate this with the timing of the first/second shot. Frame by frame analysis was also used to determine timing sequences for the firings of the three bullets.

FaAA obtained aerial photographs of Dealey Plaza as well as photographs of each building in the Plaza to assist in the creation of the computer animation of the area. The data was precise, most likely within an accuracy of approximately two inches. Using this information, the potential entry point of the President's head wound, photogrammetric positioning of the Governor and the President as well as reverse projection techniques, the Prosecution located the positions of the two men in the vehicle and then related the injury positions in the bodies. In this way, the trajectory of the bullet, i.e., the cone that you see in Posner's book, could be estimated. As you can see, there is not a straight line trajectory, but a cone, to incorporate the +− accuracy of the analysis. As the cone happens to take in all of the 6th floor window, the prosecution used this to build a strong case.

The Defense

We were able to obtain a Mannlicher-Carcano rifle and bullets from the same lot that Oswald was alleged to have fired. We concentrated on his ability as a marksman to make that shot; the quality of the weapon utilized, the "better shot" available as the vehicle moved toward the 6th floor on Houston Street, and the timing sequence of shots.

To do this analysis, we instrumented the weapon in all directions so that we could monitor the gunman's head movement as well as the rifle movement when the shots were taken. Dr. McCarthy, our CEO and an expert shot, performed the experiments as well as provided testimony during the trial. We were able to produce timing sequences that corresponded to the sequences found by the House Select Committee investigation as well as the Warren Report. In addition, we obtained skulls and attempted to reproduce the "pristine bullet." In one or two instances, a slightly damaged bullet was obtained, in others, it was heavily damaged. Dr. McCarthy also looked at using other weapons, as well as other ammunition, which might have been used to make the shots. We also located positions on the grassy knoll where witnesses alleged to have located the sounds of gunfire. In this way, we developed a "killing zone"—i.e. the first shot was taken from the 6th floor, then the vehicle moves into the "killing zone" location and the other gunmen have better shots. Remember, all we needed to do was put "doubt" in the jury's mind with regard to the facts of the case. The Prosecution had the burden of proof.

The Trial

We produced all demonstrative evidence for the trial— graphics of the scene, aerial photographs of Dealey Plaza, video of our tests, and three-dimensional animations of the Tumbling Bullet, Fly-Around of Dealey Plaza, Timing Sequence of Shots, Killing Zones, etc. The enclosed tape has a review of the trial. We hope that, as you requested, the tape will be housed in the Hood College library so that students may look at it and gain understanding on how technology can be utilized in the courtrooms of today (and the future).

The trial lasted 16 hours (2 days). It was attended by well over 500 people. We had a real jury, picked from San Francisco residents. The jury, and a shadow jury, were monitored real-time for their responses by jury consulting experts from DecisionQuest. These juries were not able to see their reactions, but the audience was. The trial was presided over by some of the most senior judges in the country, including two Federal Court Judges. Other participants besides Dr. Piziali and Dr. McCarthy were Dr. Cyril Wecht and Dr. Martin Fackler. In addition actors and members of the FaAA staff acted as witnesses. The trial resulted in 7/5 split by the jury. 7 to convict and 5 to acquit. I have enclosed a copy of the program from the event for your review of the participants.

After the Mock Trial

We were very pleased with the success of the Mock Trial and the materials that we produced. At present, continuing legal education (CLE) video tape is being produced by our organization for the ABA and its members. Everyone here has their own view of whether or not Oswald was responsible for the death of the President, but FaAA takes no position on this matter. It is my understanding that Mr. Posner contacted Dr. Piziali after he saw the Court TV show. I am not aware of what was discussed, but Mr. Posner apparently thought the prosecution's case was worth discussing and informed Dr. Piziali of such. Thus, Dr. Piziali gave approval for him to utilize their work for his investigation. We were unaware of Mr. Posner's investigation results until we saw the *US News and World Report* article last month (enclosed for your review). I have read the chapter in "Case Closed" which acknowledges the work of Dr. Piziali and his team. It is, however, a bit confusing as to the understanding that the work was done for the ABA and not Mr. Posner.

Since FaAA has not proved, or disproved anything with regard to the person (or persons) behind the assassination, we have therefore decided to make no public statements with regard to Mr. Posner's book. We leave it up to researchers, like yourself, to analyze all the facts, and myths, and draw conclusions that the rest of us can learn from.

We have received many inquiries from the national media and have been fortunate to have much of our work shown on the national networks because of Mr. Posner's reference to FaAA. If there is confusion on the part of the media when they request information from us, we correct their confusion with regard to who we performed the work for.

(Letter from Angela A. Meyer, Ph.D., P.E. to Harold Weisberg)

What she does not say is apparent: Posner did not ask Failure Analysis's permission to use its work that it did for the bar association, which commissioned it, in a book as his own work or as done for him.

I refer back to a single sentence in her letter: "It is, however, a bit confusing as to the understanding that the work was done for the ABA and not for Mr. Posner.''

"Confusing," I believe, is the very least that can be said about it. She also is probably following a Failure Analysis policy decision to make no public complaint about what Posner did in taking their work not for him and presenting it as done for him and thus his.

Although he is careful not to say so or even indicate it in his book, according to Meyer, Posner did get "approval" it seems that all he sought was some form of permission to make some kind of use of what the "prosecution" only presented to and for the ABA. As Posner both used and misused the "prosecution's" only presentation, there is no indication at all that he sought or was given permission to take Failure Analysis's work and present it as his own or as done for him. As Meyer wrote me, it is "a bit confusing as to understanding that the work was done for the ABA and not Mr. Posner."

However, there is no doubt at all that in his book Posner represents this work as his and as done for him. He also did that, quite literally, after the book was published.

What is remarkable, especially because of the great 1992 attention to that mock trial throughout most of the major media is that with the single exception of perceptive Patricia Holt's column, I know of not a single major media comment on or reporting for Posner's taking Failure Analysis's work for the ABA and presenting it as done for him, his. Holt fell short of full reporting and comment. She said only that "Posner refers to that study repeatedly but does not explain that Failure Analysis was commissioned by the American Bar Association to do that work." She does not say that Posner presents it as done for him, as his.

This presentation, while referred to as a "mock trial," was not that at all. It was much too limited to be referred to properly as a "mock trial." All that ABA asked Failure Analysis to do was "to provide all demonstrative evidence (courtboards, video, graphics, and computer animation" using "the most state-of-the-art techniques" to "educate attorneys," It definitely was not "a forum to prove or disprove that Oswald killed President Kennedy."

The definite limitation was to the three and only the three of the many elements of fact in the crime itself, as Meyer also stated. One was to the missed shot, one to "Path Trajectory of Bullets," and the third was to "Injury Analysis."

Thus it was not the need of the "defense" presentation for the purpose of educating lawyers about the new technology to make any use of it at all and it did not. The very limited presentation of the "defense" also was stated by Meyer, who was part of that team, "all we needed to do was put 'doubt' in the jury's mind."

In this, Posner deliberately suppressed from his use of the Failure Analysis presentation for and to the bar association of the fact that the preparation was for that purpose only, and with these great limitations built into it, he also suppressed that there was a defense against it and that there was a "jury" decision in which the work he uses as the only work, as definitive and beyond question, and as his or done for him was evaluated, judged. When judged, as Posner's readers, naturally, have no way of knowing, *it was found wanting. It failed!* This is the exact opposite of what Posner says. When the "defense" against what Posner used was limited to only raising "doubt" in the "jury's" mind, even with that great limitation on disputing what Posner misuses as without dispute even possible, five of the twelve jurors agreed with the "defense." And that with all the razzle-dazzle of all that gee whiz! use of the most modern computer technology.

So, and this is a further measure of Posner, in addition to presenting as *his* what Failure Analysis did for the bar association, he is as deliberately and dishonestly deceptive as he can be in pretending that the sole study was to prove Oswald guilty. And that it did. *It did not.*

All those papers and magazines that went ape for Posner and his book, all those ecstatic reviewers and their laudatory reviews, all the electronic media virtually falling all over itself to air him and sell his fraudulent book—not a word about any of this truth even though, as Meyer says, they heard from so many of "the national media." This, too, speaks for itself about our major media, shamelessly and shamefully.

Robert Kennedy misquoted Dante appropriately for this total abdication by the major media. It was something like this: "In time of moral crisis a special corner of hell is preserved for those who preserve their tranquility." Or, are silent when they should not be silent.

Of all I have seen, heard, or been told about, of all the copies of what the major media said and did when—entirely uncritically—it made itself the propagandists for the monumental fraud perpetuated on us and on the world, his Orwellian rewriting of so crucial an event in our history that had such terrible consequences, this most effective and most successful of all the efforts to protect the official miscreants, to hide what truth can continue to be hidden from the people so they cannot understand what did and did not happen when their President was assassinated, only Patricia Holt had any question at all. The record of the rest is that of a *Sieg Heil!* major media.

Still again, as at the time of the assassination throughout the official investigations, when the Warren Report was issued and throughout all the subsequent controversies, when records that had been suppressed were forced to light and in all the many court proceedings when the official "solution" was proven to be false, it failed to meet its responsibilities in a society like ours—in any society that is supposed to be free and wants to continue to be free.

As I wrote bitterly in the epilogue to my second book, *Whitewash II* (page 237), in the late summer of 1966, reporting on the past and not realizing that I was also forecasting the future, if the assassinated President had been "boll-weevil," or "a pig in interstate commerce," or "but a piece of iron, a cotton fabric or an imitation geranium," the government would have mobilized all its great power and the major media would have asked all the necessary questions if there were anything questionable at all.

As it does with a crooked petty flunky.

Can it possibly be that save for Holt, not a single reporter, reviewer or editor did not recognize that Posner had misused as his that so very well-reported ABA educational ''mock'' trial of Oswald? . . . That not one thought of pushing the right button to retrieve the *truth* while praising Posner and his book to the heavens?

What massive reporting there was to be retrieved, too. The small proportion of these printouts given to me are more than a compressed half-inch in my file. All entirely ignored by all the major media and by all the innumerable but great number of reporters, editors, and reviewers (save for Holt and later by Jeffrey Frank in the Washington *Post*), when they made an international sensation of the most deliberately dishonest book I can remember.

There is also the question of when Posner learned about it and what that then meant to him and to his book.

As noted earlier in this book, Posner's work on the book that emerged began, from what the book itself says, about a year and half before it appeared. But in his subsequent appearances Posner said that he was looking the field over with a book in mind some time earlier, perhaps, from his representations a year or a year and a half before that.

As he told *The Chicago Tribune*'s Paul Galloway in the interview that was published October 3, to begin with, ''Posner's intention was to write a primer of sorts about the assassination after examining the wealth of conspiracy theories to see what was credible and what wasn't.''

While this does not seem to be the kind of book Posner would find worthwhile or that would in any way excite Random House and encourage it to invest the time and money involved in this major effort, it certainly is not the book that appeared.

Earlier, in his Jack Sirica interview published by *Newsday* on September 16, 1993, Posner began by ''thinking that Oswald might have been part of a conspiracy involving organized crime or even a small group of friends.'' Sirica then quotes Posner as telling him, ''I believed, anyway, that Oswald had done the shooting.''

He could not have been any more specific in representing to me the purpose of his book to be nothing at all like this. He could not have been any more specific in telling me, and this was in February 1992, over that three-day period, that he was doing a book to expose the commercialism and exploitation of the assassination.

Thus, from Posner himself, we have three different books as the one upon which he was working. The real point is why does he misrepresent about something as simple as the kind of book he is writing? Why to two different interviewers after the book is out and why to one from whom he seeks help for the book he has not yet written? This is quite abnormal. The one thing that is certain, if anything ever is certain from what Posner says, is that without question he did not begin with the book that finally emerged. In the absence of what neither he nor Random House is now likely to reveal, what book was contracted, there is no way of knowing.

However, Posner himself made it clear that the book he produced is not the book that he contracted to do.

About three weeks after being closer to the truth with Sirica for *Newsday* Posner changed his approach with Galloway for *The Chicago Tribune*. That very big ego in that small man had him not even indicate to Galloway that what emerged was not his intended book at all and that the book as it appeared resulted from his own investigation and research. The quotation that follows is quoted with nothing omitted from Galloway on Posner's original intention to evaluate ''the welter of conspiracy theories'':

''Poking in the garbage

''When you read all the conspiracy books, it's apparent they can't all be right because they flatly contradict each other,'' he said. ''I knew there was garbage on the record. I didn't know how much.''

''After he debunked as many inaccuracies and false leads as he could, he assumed there would be some issues that would require further investigation, perhaps questions about acoustics or ballistics or possible Mafia involvement.

''Yet toward the end of his research, Posner notified Bob

Loomis, his editor at Random House, that he had taken an unexpected turn.

" 'I was convinced the Warren Commission had gotten it right. The evidence was overwhelming,' he said.

"Posner also was aware, of course, that a large majority of the populace thinks the Warren Commission had gotten it wrong, maybe on purpose.

"He got a feel for such skepticism when Loomis, vice president and executive editor of Random House, took his own poll at the next meeting of the publishing house's top editors, who periodically gather to report on works in progress.

" 'Bob told them about what I'd found and asked how many believed the Warren Commission was right,' Posner said. 'Remember, these are some of the brightest, best-informed, best-educated people in New York City, and no one raised a hand except Bob Loomis.'

"Posner was not dismayed. 'When people cite polls showing 70 or 80 or even 90 percent of the public as believing the assassination was the result of a conspiracy, I say I'm surprised it's not 100 percent when you consider that people have essentially heard only one side for three decades.' "

Anyone who knows anything at all about publishing, particularly on the subject of the JFK assassination, knows that it simply is not possible that Random House would have considered publishing a nothing book in which, after all the money it had contracted and advanced, the author said, "I was convinced the Warren Commission had gotten it right." There had to have been some special twist, something more than mere repetition of the official mythology. Posner does indicate that he told Loomis this and that Loomis repeated it to others at Random House: "Bob then told them about what I'd found." If Loomis had told others where he worked merely that Posner had "found" that the Warren Report "got it right" they'd have laughed in his face.

What Posner "found" and where he found it is in his aberrational half-truth to *Newsday*'s Sirica of three weeks earlier:

"Surely, the conspiracists argue, the seven entrance and exit wounds that the bullet allegedly produced had to be evidence of more than one shooter. To some reviewers, Posner's account of the path of the bullet is among the most persuasive material in "Case Closed."

"In examining the bullet's trajectory, Posner leaned on modern technology that was unavailable to the commission. Although his personal research already was leading him to conclude that the bullet did indeed pass through both Kennedy and Connally, he became a true believer after stumbling across the work of Failure Analysis Associates, a Menlo Park, Calif., engineering firm that specializes in computer recreations of accidents for use in negligence cases. The firm had done computer imaging of the Kennedy assassination for a Court TV mock trial of Lee Harvey Oswald last year.

"After seeing the show, Posner contacted the company, which allowed him to use its computer modeling in the book. . . ."

In the last quoted sentence the "company" referred to is Failure Analysis. As Meyer wrote me, Posner did not ask the "company" to allow him to use its work. He asked Piziali. And as was reported publicly, Piziali was not even an employee of Failure Analysis. He worked for "Spectus Technologies, Inc., a subsidiary of The Failure Group," as a copyrighted "PR Newswire" account of July 24, prior to the presentation to the ABA convention states. Posner says he "stumbled" onto the Failure Analysis work in its telecasting on Court TV. If that is how he blundered into it then it is to wonder what he was really investigating and researching that all the major national attention to the fact that the ABA convention would include a "mock trial" of Lee Harvey Oswald did not get his attention in any way?

Meyer's letter does confirm that it was after Posner "saw the Court TV show" of the "mock trial" at the ABA convention that he told Piziali that his "prosecution case was worth discussing."

It is apparent that what Posner excited Loomis with is that he could misrepresent this as the truth yielded by modern technology. The lawyer in Posner, clear on the dishonesty he intended that is basic to his formula, got Piziali's verbal agreement to use Failure Analysis's work for what Meyer refers to as "discussion" in his book.

Whatever that verbal agreement was, and Posner the lawyer knew that Failure Analysis would not want to litigate when there was any kind of agreement, Posner not only presented the Failure Analysis work as his own, he was careful not to include in his book that he had permission to use it. If he had to have permission to use it, obviously he could not have represented that it was his; done for him.

Posner's end notes do not even refer to personal contact with Piziali. (Pages 554–5.) They hold a single reference to Piziali's appearance at the mock trial and nothing else at all.

The catalogue of Posner's misrepresentations, all carefully plotted, still is not complete. If it can ever be complete. In his 600 pages he had no space to refer to any mock trial at any ABA convention. So, his readers were not only given the false impression that Failure Analysis's work was for him, he gives no reason even to suspect that it could have been for any other purpose or for anyone else.

Thus, too, the added Posner misrepresentation by omission in not reporting that there was any defense against what he selected to use of what Failure Analysis presented at that "trial" and thus he was able to deceive his readers and to corrupt history's record on both the import of what he used, how credible it was found to be when tested before a jury, as well as on the fact that it was intended to be only extremely limited in application and above all, not as even addressing Oswald's guilt or innocence by Failure Analysis. Atop all these and others Posner, naturally, with the basic dishonesty of his approach and of his misuse of the Failure Analysis work, had no reason to include, after all, he had only 600 pages, the fact that it all failed in the terms in which he misuses it.

It did not convince the jury: the *Journal* of the bar association headlined its account, "July Deadlocks in Oswald Mock Trial."

Posner knew this at the outset because he had his first knowledge of any of this not from his own research or investigation because as he indicated to Sirica and as Meyer told me, he saw telecast "the Court TV show." It reported the *entire* proceeding and it repeated that airing a number of times. The jury's decision was also reported nationwide by the media. All these accounts highlight Posner's calculated dishonesty; a dishonesty that appears to be the only means by which he could get Loomis and Random House to accept his alteration of what that book was to be. What follows is typical of the reporting Posner does not use in his book and pretends does not exist, knowing better, knowing the truth. This should be considered along with the stated intention of the very limited and carefully defined purpose of the entire thing, as Meyer reported it officially for Failure Analysis.

In its "final edition" of August 12, 1992, the day after the mock trial, *USA Today* headlined its account, "Hung jury in Oswald trial." The third sentence in this account is that "the results were inconclusive: The jury deadlocked after two and a half hours: seven jurors voting guilty, five to acquit."

This is not Posner's account so effectively distributed and promoted throughout the entire world by Random House. He says only the exact opposite. The five "balked" because: "The theory that Oswald fired a single, magical bullet was unbelievable; his motive for killing Kennedy was unclear; many doubts remain."

This is an entire disproof of Posner's entire book, that whole phony concoction he fabricated beginning with what he misrepresented Hartog's opinion of the boy as a born assassin and winding up with his misrepresentation of both the purpose and meaning of the one side of the Failure Analysis presentation he used and misused. The jury itself refused to accept what Posner himself represents as beyond any question at all, as absolutely unquestionable.

The very conservative *Washington Times* of the same day concluded its story, "The trial's purpose wasn't to reach a definitive verdict, but to demonstrate advances in the age-old art of lawyering."

Elizabeth Risberg's story of that day for the Associated Press, which blankets the country and the world, begins, "Even hi-tech computer animation couldn't help jurors at a mock trial decide whether Lee Harvey Oswald assassinated John F. Kennedy." She among the many others who reported that presentation and the jury's "not guilty" verdict in its hanging on the vote, reports that the "defense" was by Wall Street lawyers from Posner's old firm, and by those at the top of it, the very best lawyers and senior partners at Cravath, Swaine and Moore!

One of them, David V. Boies, said after that entire presentation that Posner later used and misused that the prosecution "hadn't met its burden of proof." Boies was not alone of the best lawyers in the firm that kept Posner working for it for so short a period of time and from his own account, where he boasted of his mind being perfect for analysis, in the most menial chore of going over discovery evidence, a chore assigned by some of the major corporations to those who do not even have a law degree, as I know from having friends who had no law training doing that for years.

Thomas Barr, Cravath senior partner quoted in *The San Francisco Chronicle* August 11 story, said, "There should be the slightest doubt of any kind as to what the facts are. And yet every single fact of any significance is open to serious doubt."

Not in Posner's version. Still another of the top partners in the firm that did not need Posner's continued services or his fabled "analytical mind," Evan Chesler, joined his associates at the firm and in the ABA's presentation of the defense at the mock trial in saying that "no one can be sure about how many shots were fired or where they came from. Despite all the evidence, the government only has circumstantial evidence to string together ... The doubts are such that in this case (the government) cannot carry its burden."

This is the exact opposite of Posner's representation of that Failure Analysis work he used as his and that opinion could not have come from better, more respected, more establishmentarian lawyers than those at the top of the firm Posner had such a short association with, although he inflated his menial role into his being a publicity and cover-worthy "Wall Street lawyer."

Let us now return to Patricia Holt's "Between the Lines" column in the September 5, 1993, *Chronicle:*

When Court TV asked Failure Analysis chief executive officer, who was part of the "defense" team and testified at the "trial" this question, "Few sharpshooters, much less Oswald, could hit a moving target as rapidly as Oswald supposedly did—can it be done?" Rogan McCarthy replied, "I can't. I'm the best shot I know. I can't do that."

Posner preferred the opinion of that good ol' boy Sergeant Zahm to the official opinion of the Marine Corp Commandant, that Oswald was a "rather poor shot," and to palm this off he suppressed the *published official report* from his book. Thus Posner could also quote Zahm's opinion that the shooting attributed to Oswald was easy. Posner suppressed the fact that the best shots the NRA could provide, all holding the very highest rating, of "master," could not duplicate the shooting attributed to Oswald—and that under greatly improved conditions. One of those several improvements was shooting at a stationary, not at a moving target. Both Court TV's host, Brian Banmiller, and McCarthy, whose professional qualifications greatly exceed Posner for a professional opinion and whose shooting skill greatly exceeded Oswald's says he could not do it; this is still another reason Posner had to suppress the fact that there was a defense and a jury verdict.

From merely the half-hour videocassette Meyer gave me there are many other reasons Posner did not dare use all of that production. Of these I here cite only a few:

It made no sense to use such a piece of junk as an assassination weapon.

JFK was shot while hidden from Zapruder's camera by the sign before Posner theorizes he was and his reaction to it is not that as fancy as the urologist, John Lattimer, but is in reaction to that shot. (Lattimer's first attempt to use "science" to prove his preconception that Oswald was the lone assassin was to slice sample bullets crosswise in his laboratory, with precision equipment with the conclusion he has not repeated since then to my knowledge). . . .

The prosecution acknowledgment that there were only three shots is mere conjecture. . . .

The time added for the shooting by additional theorizing, that 8-second scenario, is not Posner's; it is the prosecution's, and he picked that up from the Failure Analysis presentation to the bar association convention. . . .

The computer's projected path of that magic bullet through both JFK and Governor Connally in fact shows it deflected to the President's right on leaving his neck.

And where it allegedly went through his neck it was low enough to have had to go through the shirt and tie, neither of which was struck in the front by any bullet, from the official evidence itself.

Why McCarthy, Failure Analysis's CEO, did not respond to my letters I do not know. Meyer indicates that all correspondence was routed to her, that response was her official responsibility. In any organization this is comprehensible, not really unusual. I wrote McCarthy because I wanted to be able to quote what he and Failure Analysis said with complete accuracy. Neither the organization nor McCarthy had a policy of not responding for quotation. He was quoted by the media and he did agree to be quoted when my friend David Keck questioned him for direct quotation in a review of Posner's book.

Dave had been studying the subject for some years. He teaches history at the Dublin Ohio High School. He lives in Westerville, not far from that school. With his permission to quote him and with what he himself quotes within quotation marks he sent me a memorandum covering his interviews with McCarthy and several others. His conversation with McCarthy was on Monday, September 13. He also spoke about Posner's book to Cyril Wecht on September 18. As we have seen, Wecht was also involved in the ABA mock trial as an expert. He is both a lawyer and a forensic pathologist. He is the former head of the American Academy of Forensic Science.

Dave's memorandum quotes Wecht on his conversation with McCarthy in which McCarthy "confirmed that Posner never consulted with or met with them. They sent him a courtesy summary of the mock trial information." More, "Posner never commissioned them or paid them a penny." Wecht said that McCarthy "was very angry with Posner that clear inference (was made) on interviews that he commissioned them to do it." He further quotes McCarthy as saying, "This was done as a project, (with) no unanimity of opinion amongst them ... Posner is a writer and a lawyer—what he's done can't be attributed to sloppiness."

Dave's memo continues with his own words in which he also quotes McCarthy: "Regarding the allegations that Posner implied that he commissioned Failure Analysis: Posner has 'consciously attempted to create that Image!.' " Then, " 'We are terribly amused at this concept of "case closed." ' "

For the prosecution, McCarthy, of the defense team, told Dave, "There are bigger problems than the wounds."

As we have seen, those that Posner did not deal with unfaithfully in various ways and degrees he just ignored to help him declare, as he did, "Case Closed."

One problem with that rifle, as I knew from my duplicate of it on the local range, as McCarthy said, "It is a 'high energy rifle' with a 'pretty fair kick.' " Those who fired mine on the range found the kick, the recoil that thrusts the butt of the rifle strongly into the shoulder and "kicks" the muzzle end strongly upward, to be quite strong. Especially in using a telescopic sight this makes more of a problem of getting the target back into the lenses of the scope to sight and then fire. It takes more time, the amount more varying with the experience of the shooter, and it should be recalled Oswald is never known to have fired that rifle a single time so he could not know about and adjust for that strong kick.

McCarthy also told Keck as Holt quoted him, good a shot as he is, "I couldn't duplicate it," referring to the shooting attributed to Oswald. And McCarthy is an experienced, practicing rifleman.

Dave also noted some of Posner's glaring errors that I skipped. One that amused me for that pretended know-it-all Posner is that with regard to a man said to have "confessed" to being one of those utterly irrelevant "tramps" in those pictures, Posner refers to him as "Charles 'Buddy' Harrelson."

The name, Dave says, is "Charles Voyd Harrelson." He says that "Buddy Harrelson was an infielder for the New York Mets."

Wecht made a trenchant observation, referring to that really zany concoction of Posner's, that the bullet that missed and he says was the very first shot fired, in order to have the jacket and core separate so that in Posner's ignorant interpretation of what he says the FBI lab's report on the impact on that curbstone means, hit a twig or branch of a tree. That, in Posner's imagination, required for his scenario to have any possibility at all, is so that the traces the FBI got from that curbstone could be attributed to the core of that bullet. The FBI tested a concrete paste patch over the chip made by that impact, not the deposit left in that chip. But as Wecht observed, that bullet "breaks Connally's rib and radius (the heavy wrist bone), and doesn't separate but hits twigs and separates."

Obviously, for Posner's fabrication to make his theory possible (and it is only a theory), he had to make this improbability have the semblance of possibility. He writes about it for all the world as though it is real. A little twig caused the jacket to separate itself from the lead core but smashing Connally's rib and wrist bone did not! Ridiculous indeed!

History teacher Dave Keck, the baseball fan, and Cyril Wecht, of the most impeccable professional credentials as a forensic pathologist—at opposite extremes—underscore each in his own way, the arrogance of mind, the self-concept that makes real of the unreal to Posner so he puts it on paper.

The Keck and Wecht observations reveal a different kind of dishonesty than Posner employed to make his book what it is, what he could not possibly have done without all his more serious, unequaled, I think unprecedented dishonesties of which none is more essential to his book than his knowing false pretense that the Failure Analysis work was done for him and that he faithfully reported that work in his book.

With the most thoroughgoing contempt for all concepts of decency, honesty, fairness and even of normal standards of personal behavior, and with total disregard for our history and popular understanding of it as he so falsely rewrites it, he did more, ever so much more than any one person. His, the grossest and most consciously dishonest and false account of it, was accepted internationally and by our own negligent and uncaring media. They made him a famous hero and a fine public servant for it.

Quite aside from Posner's raping of all the fine traditions of the honorable craft of writers in a society like ours, a society whose proper functioning depends on the people being honestly informed, he once again gave the major media an opportunity to refuse to meet its obligations as, it has from the moment those terrible shots were fired in Dealey Plaza, failed itself and all of us again.

VI
Never Again—Again

Like Posner, Random House, and the CIA, The Failure Group also exploited the JFK assassination for its own purposes. Unlike the Posner cabal, it intended no exploitation of the assassination. It did what it had been asked to do by the American Bar Association itself, to be presented at that year's bar convention. Both intended what they regarded as a legitimate, scientific demonstration and a constructive one at that, giving nothing else any thought. Aside from the misuse Posner et al. made of it, and that is very hurtful to the country, to our history, and to people's understanding of one of the most tragic and costly events in our history, misuses that The Failure Group never intended, expected, or even thought about, the proper and intended use, although it influenced immeasurably fewer people, had the same effect.

Inherent in the concept is that in a short while, given their fine educations and experiences, such a group as the many doctors of philosophy in various disciplines as are in The Failure Group can grasp and utilize all knowledge on anything and everything and by passing what they have through all their marvelous gadgets and gismos evolve the absolute truth.

Perhaps that is true with what started The Failure Group

off to its great success and fine international reputation, like determining what caused oil-well catastrophes.

This is not true of the JFK assassination and it is not true of what was presented to the bar convention.

There is a difference between presenting to the courts what is of absolute dependability with regard to great natural catastrophes and other accidents and major political events and crimes. While there is no difference in the requirements of justice, there is an enormous difference in the capabilities of the scientific technologies in achieving justice, the ultimate objective of the judicial system.

The technologies themselves are breathtakingly marvelous. But, they are limited by what they are given to process.

These technologies can and do, if used properly, process what they are given. They do not and cannot process what they are not given to process.

There is, too, a vast difference between a simple demonstration of capabilities and uses to a limited professional audience that understands it is being given only a demonstration, and permitting widespread use in an entirely different context and to an entirely different audience for enormously different purposes.

With what The Failure Group and the American Bar Association intended this difference only begins with permitting Court TV to give a nationwide audience what only closed-circuit TV was appropriate for.

Court TV is not limited to an audience of lawyers with the need to know what can influence the justice that is the end of all legal proceedings.

Any demonstration, intended only as a demonstration, on any of the most intensely controversial national issues, like the assassination of a President, should have been limited strictly and firmly to the intended audience. The ABA could have done this. Doing this, however, denied the ABA access to most of those it wanted to reach, lawyers who would not be at the convention. Using TV to reach them, going public with the demonstration not intended for any use other than educating lawyers, where the subject matter was so intensely both political and controversial, virtually enticed misuse, especially with the thirtieth anniversary of the assassination coming.

Neither the bar association nor The Failure Group appears to have given this any thought or to have been aware of the misuses they made possible by using TV. In this they give nationwide public access to what without any reasonable question at all they intended as only an educational demonstration to a limited audience of lawyers only.

Without this serious error in judgment Posner's commercializing of it to enrich himself and recreate our history by means of it would not have been possible and there would not have been this need to attempt to correct his misuse of it to corrupt our history.

What is simply ghastly to me is that such a group of the very best, most highly educated minds in the country, with so high a percentage of advanced degrees, could begin such a project with what, to me, is the most astounding ignorance.

There seems to be no reason not to believe that Meyer is both truthful and without exaggeration in writing me that Failure Analysis Associates is "the nation's leading consulting firm dedicated to investigation, analysis and prevention of failures of an engineering or scientific nature. Our work is well known throughout the litigation field and we pride ourselves on utilizing the most state-of-the-art techniques in engineering analysis and demonstrative evidence preparation. This is why we were contacted by the ABA."

Yet, when they were approached in March 1992 by the ABA "to assist with a mock trial presentation for their 1992 annual convention" and there was "much discussion," Meyer did not say by whom but implies it was within Failure Analysis, "the decision was made to put Lee Harvey Oswald on 'trial' at the event." She added that the "Mock Trial" was "designed to educate attorneys on proper trial techniques as well as the technologies to display demonstrative evidence." She emphasized the word "educate."

For this objective, with only the time between March and early August to encompass the information and then to process it "utilizing the most state-of-the-art techniques," with what did they start, what was the source of their information to be so processed: "Both sides utilized the following background information: Warren Commission Report, House Select Committee Report, 'Crossfire' as well as a copy of the Zapruder Film." In addition, either side could with the approval of the other side, use other materials. Meyer added, "This is how we acquired your books. [John] Lattimer's medical work was also used extensively and we had discussions with Larry Howard in Dallas as well."

Given the stated purposes and intentions, in this field in which I do qualify as an expert, there could hardly have been more of the "garbage-in-garbage-out" that is the bugaboo of computering.

Probably nobody at Failure Analysis, and this gets to an irremedial flaw in such political projects, had the remotest idea that their two basic sources were fiercely partisan, intending and designed to reach a predetermined conclusion. Each was angled that way and each did precisely that in those two official reports. Moreover, the Warren Report's conclusions are not able to survive comparison with the evidence on which it is allegedly based.

But even getting my books was an afterthought. The project began with only one-sided basic information and from what evolved never escaped that one-sidedness. It will be absolutely clear that what evolved and was presented as evidence is entirely refuted by what is in the earliest pages of my very first book.

While for the limited intended use and that limited to the in-hall audience these flaws may not have invalidated the ultimate presentation, for any other use there could hardly have been any greater irresponsibility. Limiting the basic information to partisan political sources, absolute one-sidedness in this, or to the incredible trash in Jim Marrs's, (Crossfire), incompetent and grossly inaccurate compendium of all the assassination nuttiness reflects this.

This irresponsibility was by the most highly educated professionals who have amply earned, fine international reputations, too.

In it they completely validated that computering bugaboo, GIGO, garbage in, garbage out.

This with the subject the assassination of a *President?*

With all that means and all the additional controversy over what officialdom they did and did not do?

This with what inevitably had the effect of a coup d'état in our country?

And then to first permit—indeed, prearrange—for nationwide telecasting and repeated retelecasting and then to no matter how indirectly permit Posner's misuse of it and on learning of his misuse before he could make that misuse not to assert the right to prevent it? There was at the very least a common-law copyright on that presentation.

Neither the bar association nor The Failure Group asserted that ownership or made any effort at all to prevent or even influence in any way the grossest misuses Posner made of it.

This is separate from Posner's false pretenses about it, representing it as work done for him or his work.

And even when it appeared there was no protest, no effort to correct his misrepresentations of any kind about it.

Why? Only The Failure Group can say. But what is apparent is that it benefited considerably from that vast international attention. It was content to get the benefits of this misuse, without any thought at all to the great national harm from that misuse.

It is not necessary to demonstrate all the factual errors and all the harmful conclusions drawn from them, and then it was presented to one of the very greatest if not the greatest of audiences ever obtained by a vicious, dishonest book on any subject to demonstrate the unavoidable GIGO that was built into the presentation. For the certain harmful consequences of any misuse of it by anyone at any time, as Posner was permitted to make, the bar association and The Failure Group are jointly and individually responsible.

Separate from what Failure Analysis produced are what Posner did with it; that is, the opposite of what it represents, means, and says.

And considerations of Oswald's guilt must begin by putting him where it was impossible for him to be the assassin. This means placing him at that sixth-floor window to which Posner and others give provocative and prejudicial names like "sniper's den" or "nest," in time to fire that rifle by 12:30 P.M., when the motorcade passed with the rifle ready to use.

They are not able to do this, despite their contrary representations. There were, in fact, five fewer minutes for any planning of the assassination from that window or by Oswald because the motorcade was due there five minutes earlier. It was running five minutes late. That no assassin could plan on.

One hundred percent of the evidence is that Oswald did not bring the rifle to and into the building that morning.

This gets to a basic Failure Analysis error in using the Warren Report rather than also its twenty-six volumes of appendix as basic information.

All the basic research was done for it in my first book, with all the Commission sources cited in it. Failure Analysis had no work at all to do on this. The work was done for it and that work was in its hands.

The Report states what all of the Commission's own underlying, evidence states is not true. Even if Meyer meant to include those volumes, as she did not, in the accounting of the source material used, the fact still remains that Failure Analysis's prosecution team had to get that rifle into that building that morning and the Commission's own evidence precludes that.

Failure Analysis could not use a conclusion, correct or incorrect, to "educate" lawyers for their courtroom uses when the rules of evidence preclude using conclusions as evidence.

But even if that is forgotten and it is presumed in the face of all the evidence that Oswald did somehow get that rifle into that building, it then would have been disassembled and a skilled FBI expert, which Oswald was not, required six minutes to assemble the two parts of the rifle with a dime, this being used in the test because there is no indication of Oswald's access to a screwdriver.

In turn this meant that to be in that window in time to shoot, Oswald had to have been at that window before 12:24. To this must be added the time required for him to get there from wherever he was. Nobody planning any assassination and knowing anything at all about the rifle to be used could allow as little time as the best time the FBI expert could make to get that rifle reassembled. This means that Oswald had to have gotten to that window even earlier. He did not. This is established by the fact that Carolyn Arnold saw him on the first floor much later, at about 12:25. FBI records, too, reflect the fact that he could not have been at that window to do this shooting.

Forgetting that, and for the moment, forgetting any proof that Oswald did fire that rifle at that time (and there is no such proof), his escape has to be accounted for for it to have been possible within the time permitted by the official evidence. Posner reproduces the Failure Analysis graphics on this on pages 480 and 481.

This visual does reflect what has to have happened, that Oswald handled that rifle, at two additional points; when he left his supposed shooting point and when he neared where he allegedly cast it aside. Each drawing shows what he had to do; that he held the rifle. He had to have left prints when he fired the rifle, he had to have left other prints when he held it differently on leaving that window, and he had to have held it still differently in getting rid of it, leaving still other prints. Yet there were no fingerprints on that rifle consistent with this handling and, as the drawings reflect, he had to have had contact with parts of the rifle capable of accepting fingerprints.

Oswald's "assumed route" as it is reflected in the visual that Posner used is a straight diagonal from the southeastern to the northwesternmost corners of that building. This was assumed because it was necessary to make the assumption to reduce even by only seconds the time that imagined escape took. But it was a well-known and absolute physical impossibility. That floor was part of the warehouse. As existing pictures show there were stacks of books all over it and some of those stacks were higher than a man.

The dishonesty of all of this gets greater when Failure Analysis gets to where it, like officialdom, says that Oswald got rid of that rifle, only it did what officialdom did not dare do, it entirely eliminated the barricade of books behind which that rifle was hidden. This is not a pardonable oversight, if there is such a thing on such a project. Aside from the testimony and those Commission volumes they had my *Whitewash*. It discusses this escape in detail and with the official evidence only. It is indexed and it even includes one of the Commission's very poor photographs of the rifle in position where it was later found (on page 211). In any of the poor pictures and in the testimony of the officer who found it, it is apparent that unlike the "reconstructions," including that by Failure Analysis, the rifle was not merely cast aside while in flight. It was very carefully placed inside that square barricade of stacked boxes—from none of which any fingerprint was lifted—set carefully on the floor in a position from which it could not have been jarred over by accident, on the extreme rear tip of the butt and the extreme forward end of the muzzle. It also was carefully covered, with both cardboard and paper, and as Constable Seymour Weitzman testified, it was even more covered over when it was first seen than later, when the pictures were taken.

As there is no accounting for how that barricade of cartons was surmounted twice without a single fingerprint being detected, there also is no accounting for the time required for that careful hiding of the rifle, not by the Commission, not by the FBI, not by Failure Analysis, and not by Posner.

These "oversights" are indispensable because of when Oswald was seen on the second floor and because in all reconstructions it is necessary to have him outside the building by 12:33.

With all the deliberateness of all the so-called reconstructions it still was not possible to get Oswald to and into that second-floor lunchroom before he would have been seen outside of it by the building manager, Roy Truly, who was rushing up those stairs ahead of police officer Marrion Baker.

Oswald was inside that lunchroom—the door to which had an automatic closer and with a Coke in his hand when Baker saw him through the small window in the door, he said, and when Truly, ahead of Baker and farther up the stairs, did not see either him or the door close.

There is not and never had been any legitimate question about this: the evidence not only did not place Oswald where he could have fired any shots from that sixth-floor window—the evidence proves he could not have been there to do it. No matter how special interests may contort and misrepresent it, *this is the official evidence* and it is the closest thing there is to real evidence, nobody having seen Oswald from before the shooting until Baker saw him inside that lunchroom.

The picture of the rifle as hidden in itself is enough to disprove the official and those semi-official "solutions" based on Oswald firing from that window.

Here is the true "Case Closed."

The appendix part of the *U.S. News* use of the Posner book begins exactly as Posner has that appendix begin in the book, with one exception: *U.S. News* actually asserted a Posner copyright on Failure Analysis's work.

At the bottom of the magazine's page 88 is this line, in capital letters: "ADAPTED FROM THE FORTHCOMING BOOK 'CASE CLOSED: LEE HARVEY OSWALD AND THE ASSASSINATION OF JFK' BY GERALD POSNER." This is followed by the copyright symbol and that is followed by, referring to the copyright, "BY GERALD POSNER, PUBLISHED BY RANDOM HOUSE, INC."

Failure Analysis also distributes copies of the reprint from the magazine with the copyright on its work claimed in Posner's name!

Posner hates to refer to "the magic bullet," part of his pretense that there was no such thing, although he himself has introduced real magic, as in that tree that he says stripped the bullet core of its casing and then redirected the core alone in two different directions. So he heads his version of some of Failure Analysis's work "Appendix A" while when Random House sold the serialization rights to the magazine it had the "Magic Bullet" headline in large type.

Each version begins with the identical picture with similar captions. In the book the caption is "This is the single bullet that wounded both JFK and Connally." In the magazine the caption is "bullet that hit JFK and Connally: true size." In the book this is presented as Posner's picture, his work. The magazine has credit to "National Archive." But in each the picture is identical. It consists of a side view of the bullet, which is vertical, and a short distance below the bottom is an "end view" of its base. In neither version is it possible to make any sense out of the view of the base. If this were not significant for other reasons, as it is, it would still be true because the end view is so small and so unclear nothing can be made out of it of what is there to be made out. From side to side in this version the bullet, slightly compressed, is less than a quarter of an inch across. As I published two different photographs of the same base of the same bullet on the same page, 602, of *Post Mortem,* the narrower of the two I published is more than eight times the size of what Failure Analysis used, a full two inches wide compared with less than a quarter of an inch.

What Failure Analysis (and Posner—and *U.S. News*) obscured with so small a picture is all of the evidence held by the base of that bullet. It also failed to explain the difference between the picture of the base of the bullet it published and that I did, mine having also been taken for me by the National Archives.

There is a black dot in the picture of the base Failure Analysis used and Posner took from it and also used. There is no explanation for the addition of any dot to the picture. Of the possible explanations what seems most likely is that after Vincent Guinn drilled out a sample for his testing for the House Assassinations Committee, when photographed the hole appears to be solid black.

If this is true then we have still another view of what it takes to be and to act as a great scientific expert dealing with evidence! With the rest of the entire base of the bullet entirely untouched, Guinn drilled his hole of only about a single millimeter in diameter slap down in the middle of what then was obscured in pictures, where the FBI removed a relative massive sample for the postage stamp weight, a single millimeter in length specimen, all that is necessary for spectographic analysis!

My authority for saying that this is all that is required for spectrographic analysis is the FBI lab agent who performed that very test, John F. Gallagher, when I deposed him in my FOIA lawsuit for those test results, C.A. 75–226. (This and the other depositions in that lawsuit are in the files of the court, of my attorney, Jim Lesar, who did the questioning, in the Department of Justice files, and in my own files.)

Guinn used the one place that should have been preserved precisely as it was, with all the area around the entire circumference of that base where he could have drilled his hole for his sample.

But then from Failure Analysis there is no way of knowing that any hole was drilled or that any specimen was taken. And although, as we have seen, Posner knew that Guinn had taken the sample and then Posner wrote quite deceptively about that, he makes no mention of this in the caption with that picture even though the entire text of that page is his, not Failure Analysis's.

How Failure Analysis was going to "educate" lawyers for the bar association, especially as in this instance, criminal lawyers, without showing that the specimens that are removed so radically and so unnecessarily altered that evidence and its meaning, and that misuses are possible with what is removed and is not accounted for, only it can try to explain.

How it did not "educate" criminal lawyers to ask questions about such untoward official treatment of evidence Failure Analysis can also try to explain, as it does not. But then it does not mention that Guinn himself certified, covering his own ass, that the official specimens he tested do not match their official descriptions in any way. He nonetheless proceeded with his charade of an expert testing for expert testimony.

What this says and means is important to understand in this matter and as commentary on professional experts who testify.

Guinn knew the specimens he was given to test did not match their official descriptions. He even said he did not know what happened to those official specimens. But he nonetheless went ahead and tested what he had been given, knowing they were not the actual specimens described, and then reported on his tests of them as though they were the official specimens he said they were not.

Guinn also testified that the specimens he tested were remarkably identical in their composition.

Now if by any chance the FBI, which was careful not to

keep any records, including the weight of the core material it removed from the base of that bullet, had for any reason, by accident or design, substituted for the actual specimens material it removed from the base of that bullet, then, of course, it would test identical, as Guinn emphasized it did.

Examination of the bullet base in the pictures I published where the minimum width of the quarter-inch bullet is so greatly magnified makes it apparent that there is no other area of that base from which any fragments could have been shed in the course of its officially conjectured meteoric career. All the rest of it is of unblemished smoothness.

With this for beginnings ought not some lawyers sure as hell be getting an education? Albeit not the education intended by the bar or the scientists?—without any mention of it by the bar or by the scientists? Could not a competent criminal lawyer get an acquittal on this alone?

Posner's appendix A's next two pages, unnumbered 474 and page 475, also used identically by *U.S. News* on pages 78 and 79, is the Failure Analysis spread on the rifle. The text is identical in each but the magazine set and used its own type.

(The most likely explanation of Random House's inability to get the word "appendix" and the page numbers on some pages is that it used Failure Analysis's work so literally it photographed it and that left no space on some pages for the word and numbers.)

It is immediately apparent that Posner got "his" eight-second total time for that shooting and "his" "solution" that has the first shot miss, not the second shot, from Failure Analysis, too. It is on his unnumbered pages 474, photographed from Failure Analysis's work, leaving no space for either his "appendix" identification or its number!

While this version of what Failure Analysis evolved gives no reason even to suspect that the first shot missed, as we have seen fifteen-year-old David Lui did that for Posner who, in return, absolved Lui for any responsibility by presenting it as his work, not the boy's.

And, although Failure Analysis also attributed its ability to make this conjecture to "Enhancements of the Zapruder film," little Lui did that without any enhancement and from a poor copy of that same film.

(Who needs enhancements when they have little Lui?)

Under "Bolt Action," Failure Analysis has four sketches of it to illustrate how bolt-action works on a rifle. It has this caption for its explanation: "The bolt action can easily be executed in a fraction of a second." From my own experience from the official testing "easily" is not true. The action is stiff and it sometimes hangs.

Before the bolt action could be operated at all that rifle had to be *removed* to prevent the eye from being put out by the bolt as it is withdrawn because of the scope.

That rifle was not designed for the use of a scope!

Aside from the fact that that particular rifle has a history of sticking, which prevents the bolt from being operated at all until that is overcome, the *official* record of the *official* test firing, set forth in my *Never Again!* (its sole source is the *official* testimony relating to the experience of the "masters," the best shots in the country with that rifle), in that testimony Posner said he had to index to get access to it although this is included in the Meagher index he found to be so "political"), is the exact opposite of what Failure Analysis says! Posner and *US News,* too!

Each and every one of those "masters" found the bolt action difficult, not "easy" to use, and, together with that rifle's mule kick, *they all missed on their second shot with it.* They had to adjust to the difficulty of that bolt action in firing, and that is, remember, with the country's very best experts. This is not what is said with that illustration, that "the bolt action can easily be executed in a fraction of a second."

As Piziali's pippin science continues on the next page, Failure Analysis says that in the Marines, Oswald was "proficient with an M–1 rifle (with which the Mannlicher-Carcanno, as is not said here, can hardly be compared) at distances up to 200 yards." The truth is that when Oswald did that firing, as again the official evidence shows, he was so lousy a shot his mates doctored his score so he would qualify, and even then he barely did. This is outside of Failure Analysis's consideration. Quoting again, with nothing omitted in quotation "without the benefit of a telescopic sight."

Who says that with that rifle and that shooting a telescopic sight was a benefit? For one capable of hitting the President in the head at that distance, not at all a great distance for a rifle, under any conditions a scope, is a liability in that it does, under the best of circumstances, take more time to get on target than using open sights does. But with *that* rifle, having to take the rifle down to operate the bolt without damage to one's self is a "benefit" in *rapid* fire? It is not!

Next Failure Analysis alleges that a sling that did not fit and could not be used as a rifle sling is ordinarily used, a sling said to have been "adapted from the belt of a Navy pistol holster," when the official evidence says no such thing at all, "provided additional steadiness."

Yet on the very same page Failure Analysis has a drawing of Oswald firing that rifle resting it on a stack of cartons *without using that sling*!

Can that rifle be operated from that position with a sling and then not have to slip off the sling to be able to operate the bolt and then slip it back into place? Does this not take more time when fractions of a second are precious?

And does the sling in fact provide any "steadiness" at all over and above what is provided by the conjectured stack of cartons on which the rifle rests?

Is it even a good idea under these conditions to use a sling that works, rather than one like this that from the official evidence itself did not work?

Failure Analysis's very next words are "A brown paper bag, 3 inches longer than the disassembled rifle, was found in the sniper's nest."

The one thing this can do to "educate" lawyers is to teach them never, ever, to trust any scientist, or any professional expert or witness at all.

This is so magical a bag it is supposed to have held that rifle while Oswald held it dependent, holding it as he walked some distance, without the rifle or his grip making any creases or other marks on that bag and, with that rifle "well oiled" (the

FBI lab's words), that magical bag had not a smidgeon, not the faintest trace of any oil on it!

Still on the same page, under "The Sniper's Nest," Failure Analysis refers to "a slight crease where the rifle ... rested when firing." Naturally it needed to cite no evidence, which is fortunate, because there is no such evidence!

Not that the crease was caused by any rifle and not that that box was even positioned where it could have been used as a rifle rest that shooting!

The one thing that is certain is that the police began moving those boxes around before any pictures of them were taken. Even then this shifting of boxes continued! To the degree that the Commission actually published at least four different and contradictory official versions of how those boxes allegedly were when the police got there when in fact, from pictures taken from the outside, all four were wrong! There may have been more than four of these pictures that the Commission published. I do not remember. But I do know there were at least four because in *Whitewash,* my first book, I published four that the Commission published on facing pages, 204–5, and they are all different.

And, as Meyer told me, the Piziali crew had that book.

But then who needs evidence when one has computers, is that it?

One more item from the same page should suffice to educate lawyers and others, hopefully also those who employ this "state-of-the-art technology," about what can be done and attributed to computers.

There are four references to Oswald fingerprints on this page: three as found on boxes and one on that magical bag:

"Left index finger and right palm prints on paper bag." Is *that* how Oswald carried that rifle inside that bag, down the Irving, Texas, streets and from the TSBD parking lot to and into that building, albeit with that bag not in his hands in any way when he entered that building? With that length package flat on his opened right palm? Steadying it perhaps in that no mean transportation accomplishment with only his "left index finger?"

And with that weight inside a bag, allegedly, if it had been carried in any other way would that magic bag have prevented the deposit of any other prints where he held it as it did prevent the deposit of oil from that rifle?

Random House has *editors*? When they pass *this* stuff without any question?

Failure Analysis *scientists* jazzed this up and others did not perceive that it is farcical, not scientific?

The location of the three remaining prints, placed on carefully sketched boxes located without any evidence—if not in contradiction to the official evidence—to suggest a sniper's nest and boxes arranged to provide a gun rest, also involves magical boxes. The sketch depicts at least three of these cardboard cartons.

The largest and with them loaded with books the heaviest of these cartons that Oswald allegedly stacked for his sniper's next and firing support has not a single print on it!

The one he allegedly lifted into place as his gun rest, filled with heavy books, remember, which on the top of its left rear as he allegedly faced it, is his "left palm print" in that very corner, exactly where not specified. He lifted that box into place with only one hand and it on top of the box when he lifted it? There is not another print anywhere on it.

Then there is an additional box for which he had no use at all, drawn in well behind where he is depicted crouching, rifle to the shoulder. It has only a "right palm print" on a corner only. He must have somehow levitated that one-handedly to put it in the place where it served no purpose for him!

How this can "educate" lawyers in any way is not apparent because those were the very cartons of boxed books with which Oswald was assigned to work, the cartons from which he removed books to fill the orders he was paid to fill.

What would have been significant is if he had left no fingerprints at all on any of them after spending that very morning filling orders from them as he had done for several preceding weeks, too!

This is "science?" Obtained by a "state-of-the-art" technology, with all that computer high-tech methodology?

If it is, when freedom and lives are to be controlled by it in the marvelous new wave of the future with which lawyers were being "educated" do we not need a law requiring that all garbage heaps be guarded around the clock so that "scientists" have no access to them?

To protect us all from "garbage in, garbage out?"

Then there is the magic of those "cones" put in place by backward projection, from two of the President's wounds, neither of which is located as precisely as is required for this to be done well, accurately, or even truthfully.

Is the rear wound in the neck or in the back? The official evidence places it both places: that single wound.

Because it is said to have exited the front of the neck, if it is assumed that it was not deflected then there are two points that can be connected and regarded as the center line of Failure Analysis's magic "cones depicting where the bullet could have come from," cones that include that infamous window but also many other points of possible origin.

However, with the fatal bullet having exploded into many pieces and having blown an appreciable portion of the head out, how can any cone be responsibly projected backward when there is no second point to make a line that can be the center of the backward projection of any cone to indicate where that shot could have originated?

Then there is the radical contradiction between the autopsy report, which places the entry of that shot low on the back of the head, and the report of the panel of the most eminent experts the Department of Justice could obtain to review the identical film evidence, pictures and X rays. With this panel placing the point of entrance four inches higher up on the head, near the top, and with the curve of the head making an increased difference if there is backward projection in the form of a cone from that entry point, when it is projected backward as far as it must be, is there not a vastly different cone covering a different area?

In Failure Analysis's cone science there is no cone for Posner's missed first bullet. Instead of a cone there is a forward projection of dotted lines, from that window to the tree that is now in our history as a magical tree. The magic comes from its separating the jacket of the bullet alleged to have hit the core, with the core only continuing after being directed in two different new directions, horizontally and vertically. Great magic indeed because, as Cyril Wecht pointed out when a sister bullet smashed four inches of one of Governor Connally's ribs and then demolished his wrist, which has heavy bones in it, it allegedly remained unscathed, with its jacket undisturbed.

The Failure Analysis projection, on Posner's page 477, projects that bullet into the *east* side of that tree, the side *away* from where its core allegedly impacted at the extreme *western* limit of Dealey Plaza.

The magic required to be added to Posner's version of its magic is what is required to navigate the core through the mass of the entire tree, with none of the many branches or twigs or even the trunk able to discourage it in its determined flight, come what may, to get down to that corner of the Plaza and enter Jim Tague into our history spraying up concrete from the curbstone to wound him slightly but to make him bleed, without removing any concrete at all from that curbstone; making it smoother instead!

Then there is the Failure Analysis treatment of ''The Single Bullet,'' Posner's both unnumbered pages 478 and 479. As drawn there is considerable distortion. As it appears on these pages this bullet seems to go crosswise inside the President and then into Connally, who is drawn considerably lower than JFK, as he was not. Why Failure Analysis did not draw this part of its ''enhancements'' looking at right angles to the victims, the only meaningful way, is not indicated. But it does depict the point of that bullet's entry well to the President's right, which contradicts all the official evidence. It shows the exit lower. This is to make the bullets imputed career inside the governor seem possible. But in its exit from JFK, confirmed by the Failure Analysis video, that bullet has to have made holes in the front of the President's shirt and tie that are not in them.

Magical shirt and collar, too?

It is on this Failure Analysis page that Posner gets his uncredited stuff, and it is stuff, on that ''Thorburn position'' magic by which he has the President's arms locked in front of him.

Here, too, is where Posner picked up that alleged "cavity caused by the bullet" that those authentic eminences of the Justice Department panel did not see and where the splintered bone from a grazed vertebra in the Failure Analysis interpretation of what the X rays show that this panel of the most eminent said unequivocally they are metal fragments. The best experts the government could get are not as good as Failure Analysis's computer whizzes? They cannot read X rays as well, with the most eminent of radiologists and the most eminent forensic pathologist reading them?

The magic does not end. It continues on the next unnumbered page, 479. There this bullet that was following the curve of Connally's rib on its inside is said to have been "slightly deflected" by that rib.

Slightly?

Downward and to the left through the wrist so that it can then, as Failure Analysis does not say, be deflected again to go for three inches, pretty much straight and just under the skin of Connally's left thigh, from his right wrist and downward into his left thigh and then forward.

With this bullet now traveling backward as it smashed that wrist, Failure Analysis ends its flight without getting it into the thigh. Perhaps that was the safest place to end this particular element of that unprecedented magic.

The backward-flying bullet's history is resumed three pages later with the earlier pictures of the side and bottom of the official bullet on the same page with a Failure Analysis test bullet, fired at a reduced charge to duplicate the imputed reduced energy of the official magic bullet. Failure Analysis says that its reduced charge test bullet emerged "in even better condition than 399," the exhibit number of the original magic bullet.

The Failure Analysis bullet did indeed emerge in better condition. It not only did not deposit the fragment in Connally's chest that the doctor in charge of his care testified under oath is there, and it did not have to discharge a sliver to go into Connally's thigh for those three inches, the sliver that remains there with the hole in the thigh much too small—according to

Dr. Malcolm Perry, called in to examine that wound—to have permitted any bullet to enter, leave or lurk there awaiting the proper moment for its emergence at the hospital, for the official account of that bullet. It left fragments in his wrist, too.

Failure Analysis's caption of this part "The Single Bullet Tested" is not exaggeration. It was most severely tested!

So tested, it flunked by the *official* evidence itself.

It would have been interesting, though, if all those scientists with all those PhDs at Failure Analysis had in some way addressed how reducing the charge of test bullets and eliminating the earlier history required by the official accounts—accounts in which that magical bullet at least had some contact with a JFK vertebra and then smashed Connally's rib for four inches—without any effect on that bullet at all, whether or not a visible effect, before its imagined course through Connally's wrist, even without its subsequent official history inside his thigh by three inches.

All those impacts had no effect on it in any way, not even on its molecules?

Failure Analysis's "science" eliminated the need to compare its test bullet with those tested for the Commission at the Army's Aberdeen Proving Ground. Those bullets, without any one tested for the full official account of its career, every single, solitary one of them was quite deformed.

We now know what wonders can be worked with "reduced charges" as well as by "backward projection" and all the other magic wrought by "state-of-the-art technology."

Is there anything at all that cannot be proved by this modern technology?

VII
Ignoring the Truth

Aside from the misrepresentations in so much of what Posner writes there is also the equally omnipresent misrepresentation by omission. The many illustrations of this in preceding chapters, notably (what with all his uninhibited chest-beating in his boasting of the CIA's great favor to him in making Nosenko available), Posner suppressed from what he claims is the most definitive biography of Oswald much that Nosenko had told the FBI and that I published in 1975, that the KGB suspected Oswald was an American sleeper agent, that he hated the USSR, that he was the worst of shooters, unable to hit even a rabbit with a shotgun, things like that, uncongenial to the new Oswald Posner created for his special purposes.

On the evidence of getting that rifle into the building in Oswald's hands that Friday morning, Posner ignores the most probative, the official evidence that he did not.

Posner was untruthful in saying that the fibers recovered from the blanket in which that rifle was allegedly wrapped were positively connected to that blanket. He knew the truth from *Whitewash*. Yet his invented "new" solution that he claims closes the case did not address the incontrovertible evidence that proves Oswald did not in fact carry that rifle into the building in the package that from all of the evidence he did not take into the building in any event. This is Posner's pattern in the next chapter, "He Looked Like a Maniac," with the subtitle: "Oswald's Escape." (Pages 263–285.)

We have seen Posner's lying to fabricate his false case by that means. Now we study his deliberate omission of solid, official evidence; evidence requiring that he omit what he knew or he destroys his contrived case. The evidence, scientific and first-person, that disproves his and the Commission's false story about Oswald's carrying that rifle into the building inside that bag serves also to introduce Posner's omissions with which this next chapter begins, how he has Oswald "escape" that building.

The Commission had to expect extensive critical reading that could or would spot gross omissions. The record on Posner is clear: he did not expect this and his judgment was correct, he did not have to face it. The major media was preconditioned to accept any support of the official mythology.

The magnitude of Posner's misrepresentations and its importance to his counterfeiting an impossible "solution" is what we now address, preparing the reader for Posner's account of Oswald's "escape" with a brief account of what he knew, omitted and got away with omitting what was really an indispensable part of his and the Commission's explanations of how Oswald supposedly got that rifle into that building, inside that special bag he is supposed to have made to hold it by stealing the paper and the tape from the depository the day before the assassination. What we quote is from *Whitewash*, which Posner had and used, and which was available to all of those who abandoned all their critical faculties and praised his book as the best of possible books on the subject.

As Pulitzer prize-winning *Newsday* reporter Patrick J. Sloyan described it in a syndicated review two columns long, with a picture from the Zapruder film included as it appeared in *The Louisville Courier Journal*, it is a "landmark book" that "is required reading for anyone interested in the American crime of the century."

As the actual evidence is laid out in *Whitewash* (pp. 22ff) it is a landmark of successful, multifaceted dishonesties that should be "required reading" for all who review controversial books:

> "The Report does not consider it necessary to do more than get Oswald to the building and into it." It dismissed the unequivocal and uncontradicted testimony of Frazier and his sister by deciding they were "mistaken." It paid even less heed to Dougherty, the only witness who saw Oswald enter the building when he said "positively" Oswald carried no package—it just ignored him in its conclusions (R137).
>
> These conclusions also state Oswald "took paper and tape from the wrapping bench of the Depository and fashioned a bag large enough to carry the disassembled rifle."
>
> Just as there is no evidence of any kind that the rifle was ever disassembled, there is no evidence that Oswald ever took any paper and/or tape. There were no eyewitnesses. There was absolutely no evidence—not even a wild rumor about either. The Commission simply decided that, because the unassembled rifle was 5.4 inches shorter, it was 5.4 inches closer to the only testimony on the size of the package. It did the same with the packaging materials. Having decided that Oswald carried the rifle into the building in a bag, despite the fact that its only evidence was exclusively to the contrary, the Commission had no problem deciding that Oswald had just taken these materials and made the bag. It does not say whether he made the bag in the building before taking it to Irving—which involved the possibility, if not the probability, of detection—or made it in Irving, which the statements by Marina and Ruth Paine would seem to eliminate as a possibility. He just made it, unseen and somewhere. Each reader may decide for himself where and how. It made no difference to the Commission. And it makes no difference, in any event, for there is no evidence that he made or used it. (Page 20.)

Omitting this, which is indispensable in his omission of what follows it, is one reason Posner had to simply ignore this and the following evidence in his supposed step-by-step account:

"Having made the bag of a material that had the remarkable quality of preserving fold markings imperishably
and accepting none other, or having just stolen this paper,
Oswald had to get the bag or the paper to Irving. The
only man who ever took him there, and without doubt the
man who took him there the evening of November 21,
was asked about both a package and about 'anything,' and
Frazier was positive in his response to both forms of the
question (2H242). And the package was much too large
to have been pocketed.

Meanwhile, the Commission's identification expert is in-
voked in a section erroneously entitled 'Scientific Evidence Linking Rifle and Oswald to Paper Bag' (R135–7).
Through FBI questioned-documents expert James C. Cadigan, the Commission established that a sample of paper
taken from the wrapping table the day of the assassination
could be identified as from the same roll as that from
which the paper for the bag came (R135;4H93). This related
no more to Oswald than to anyone else with access to the
building. But in also establishing that a roll of paper was
consumed in three days (R136), the Commission clearly
proved that Oswald could not have taken the bag and/or the
paper to Irving, for the materials could have been taken at
most two days (if, indeed, at all) before the day of the assassination. Unless, of course, it could prove that the Depository
had other rolls of paper from the manufacturer's same batch,
which it could not prove (R136). (Page 20.)

Posner was no more anxious than the Commission to explain
how Oswald could have carried and hidden paper tape that was
thoroughly wet by the time it came from the machine that dis-
penses it in those days before self-adhering tape was invented.

Mr. Cadigan's science further weakened the Commission's theory in two additional ways, which the Report
ignores. First, he established that the tape had been run
through the tape-dispensing machine. The significance of
this will become clear in discussion of the totally sup-

pressed testimony of Troy Eugene West. Then he reported on his careful scientific examination of the bag to see "if there were any significant markings or scratches or abrasions or anything by which it could be associated with the rifle . . ." The result? There were none (4H97).

The Commission found it expedient to ignore this part of its own expert's testimony on his scientific inquiry on its behalf in referring to the "Scientific Evidence Linking Rifle and Oswald to Paper Bag. (Page 20.)

This was no less expedient for Posner. His misrepresentation of what the FBI's testing of the blanket fibers, shows which follows, was known to him from *Whitewash*:

> Instead, it quoted Paul M. Stombaugh, another FBI laboratory expert, on his examination of 'a single brown delustered viscose fiber and several light green cotton fibers.' Stombaugh compared these few fibers with the blanket and found they did match some of those in the blanket. Despite this, 'Stombaugh was unable to render an opinion that the fibers which he found had probably come from the blanket . . .' " (R137.)
>
> Briefly, then, the 'Scientific Evidence Linking Rifle and Oswald to Paper Bag' did not do any such thing. It may fairly be said this 'evidence' did the opposite." (Page 21.)

(In 1986 a Paul M. Stombaugh was expelled from the USSR in an espionage scandal that also led to the expulsion of Nicholas Daniloff, correspondent of *U.S. News and World Report*. A Soviet aviation engineer, Adolf G. Talkachev, was executed. The accusation against Daniloff was that he was a courier for another alleged spy who reported to Stombaugh. In the accounts of this incident in newspapers and magazines and books I saw no recognition of the name of that expelled attaché being identical with that of the former FBI lab agent. In the book of the British reporter Tom Mangold, *Molehunt*, page 300, the expelled attaché's name is given as Paul M. Stombaugh, Jr. Mangold cites the book of one of Posner's promoters, David Wise,

The Spy Who Got Away, New York, Random House, 1988)
pages 261–2 as his source. The Warren Commission does not
list the FBI lab witness as "junior.")

The custodian of the paper and tape, Troy West, who rarely left
his wrapping table, does not entirely escape Posner's attention.
Posner refers to him as sitting and eating lunch (page 227). In this
casual mention Posner discloses that he not only knew what is here
repeated from *Whitewash* about West, but that he also read West's
testimony, citing his reading of that testimony as his source (page
541). Yet Posner says no more about West than that when he was
sitting and eating lunch he did not see Oswald. What Posner did not
burden his readers or the success of his book with is:

Custodian of the wrapping table at which these materials
are kept was Troy Eugene West (6H356–63). West had
been employed by the Book Depository for 16 years and
was so attached to his place of work that he never left his
bench, even to eat lunch. His only separation from it, aside
from the necessary functions of life (and this is presumed;
it is not in his testimony), was on arrival before work, to
get water for coffee.

He knew of no time when any employees had ever borrowed any tape or ever used it for themselves. Asked if
Oswald ever helped him or if he ever noticed Oswald
around either the paper or the tape, both of which are at
his bench, West replied: 'Never.' Asked 'Do you know
whether or not he (Oswald) ever borrowed or used any
wrapping paper for himself?' West declared, 'No, sir; I
don't.' Assistant counsel David W. Belin, conducting the
examination, repeated, 'You don't know?' and West reaf-
firmed his answer, replying, 'No; I don't.' " (6H360)

If this is not the reason the Report ignores West's testimony, what follows is equally destructive to what the
Commission wants believed. West reiterated his testimony
that, so far as he knew, no employees "ever" used or
borrowed the tape for themselves, and Belin turned to
questions about the dispensing machine itself. The Commission had already established that two of the cuts on

the tape had been made by the machine, presuming them to be the cuts at the end of a length of tape that was later torn into smaller pieces by hand. Hence, Belin wanted to know, "If I wanted to pull the tape, pull of a piece without getting water on it, would I just lift it up without going over the wet roller and get the tape without getting it wet?" West explained this would be impossible, saying, "You would have to take it out. You would have to take it out of the machine. See, it's put on there and run through a little clamp that holds it down, and you pull it, well, then, the water, it gets on it." (6H361)

Having proved that the tape on the bag had been dispensed by the machine, the Commission thus established beyond any question that the tape was wet when dispensed and had to be used immediately, if not at the bench, at least very close to it. And the man who was always there established that Oswald never was.

The only possibility remaining, an effort to get West to admit that he was away from his bench, was totally unsuccessful and had the opposite effect." (Page 21.)

Even in Posner's account of how Oswald allegedly carried that mysterious bag he has to have left many fingerprints all over it. But it was another bit of magic evidence, like the magical bullet:

"No, sir," he reiterated, "I never did hardly ever leave the first floor. That is just stayed there where all my work was, and I just stayed there" (6H362)

The only suggestion of any connection between Oswald and the bag was through fingerprints. Because Oswald worked where the bag was reported to have been found, the presence of his fingerprints was totally meaningless. Sebastian F. Latona, supervisor of the FBI's Latent Fingerprint Section, developed a single fingerprint and a single palmprint he identified as Oswald's. More significantly, "No other identifiable prints were found on the bag" (R135).

After all the handling of the bag attributed to Oswald, first in making it, then in packing it, then taking it to

Frazier's car, putting it down in the car, picking it up and carrying it toward if not into the building for two blocks, and then, at least by inference, through the building, and when removing and assembling a rifle Marina testified he kept oiled and cleaned, how is it to be explained that he left only two prints? The only thing as strange is that this bag was also handled by the police and was the only evidence they did not photograph, according to their testimonies, where found. Yet the freshest prints, those of the police, were not discovered." (Page 21–2.)

Marina's testimony was confirmed by the FBI lab. It found the rifle was well oiled.

If it were not that magic has been indispensable to Posner it might be possible that he shunned and omitted this official testimony of which he was well aware because it depends on magic; specifically we here have seen a magical paper and a magical blanket that reject the oil of the well-oiled rifle because no such oil showed in the FBI lab's testing. The paper had the added magical property of refusing to accept all the fingerprints having to have been deposited on it—if the official history of that bag is true.

Which is hardly possible.

This demonstraates how Posner creates his proofs by the overt omission of what was well known, a less polite description is by the crudest suppressions. His skilled practice of it in what he says is his account of Oswald's escape is actually essential to the possibility of the crime as Posner and the Commission state it happened.

No-Source Posner begins his Oswald escape chapter with exploiting his Hartogsian practice of mind reading. He opens it stating that Oswald had little time to prepare for what would make him famous as he so longed to be and that one evidence of this is "the fact that he had only four bullets with him, though the rifle's clip could hold six." (Page 263.) In fact the rifle could have held an aditional bullet. If Posner knew anything at all about rifles, he would have known this. That additional bullet could have been chambered before the loaded clip was inserted.

This quote reflects again Posner's gross ignorance of the established facts of the case about which he writes glibly, pretending there is nothing he does not know. How else can he say it is a "Case Closed" other than to have considered all the evidence?

His and the official mythologies are based on the same and entirely unproven conjecture, one of those things he was praised for never resorting to in those dust-jacket encomiums, the conjecture that the rifle was in the Paine garage and that Oswald got it from there the morning of the assassination and carried it to the scene of the crime in that magical bag. The problem No-Source has here is that "no kiddin' " is more than justified. Unless, as I doubt, Posner would accuse the Dallas police of planting evidence. Their search disclosed there was other such ammunition in that garage. So, there was not a blessed thing to keep Oswald from not limiting himself, albeit with utter irrationality if the official mythologies are true, to those four bullets.

In admitting what certainly casts some doubt on Oswald's expectation of getting away with what is attributed to him firing all the shots from that sixth-floor window, Posner says he "could not be certain of finding a deserted floor or area from which to shoot." Posner ends this consideration without going further, but the fact is that Oswald, most of whose work was on the floor, knew very well that it was the floor of the warehouse least likely to be "deserted" because a new floor was being laid on it. That put people there all the time other than at lunchtime and with the low wages paid, there was no certainty at all that one or more of the men paid so little would not brown-bag. Or, as Posner does not spell out, the floor with the least probability being "deserted" was the very one Oswald supposedly selected.

As part of his No-Source mind reading Posner says that "it was not a suicide mission. Oswald wanted to escape." That no doubt accounts for his leaving all but fifteen dollars of what he had for Marina, keeping an insignificant sum for any escape.

Without any other word about the crime, with which he later does toy around, disconnected from the vital evidence he here plays his special kind of games with, Posner begins the second page of this chapter (page 264):

"After firing the final shot, he slipped through the narrow gap he had created between the cartons of books. He hurried diagonally across the sixth floor, toward the rear staircase. Next to the stairs, Oswald dropped the rifle into an opening between several large boxes. It hid the gun from view unless someone stood almost directly over the boxes and peered down."

This is quite a jumble and it jerks the reader's mind quite a bit, not an unwise trick considering what Posner is up to.

It reveals his skilled practice of omission of the best evidence. He need not have left his account of how Oswald supposedly disposed of the rifle so vague when the Commission, as he certainly knew from that devoted reading of its evidence, as well as indexing it, too, had photographs of that rifle as found. They were taken by the police identification unit photographer, Lieutenant Carl Day and his assistant, Robert Lee Studebaker. Studebaker's testimony is included in what Posner read in his diligent research of all those Commission volumes. It is in Volume 7, beginning on page 137. But then Posner is prejudiced against Studebaker, or may be against crime-scene pictures, because with more than 600 pages he makes no mention of Studebaker's name. Not one time.

Of course in his own book Posner is entitled to decide for himself what pictures he wants and does not want. Posner has sixteen pages of pictures most appearing more than one picture to a page, yet for a book supposedly the most definitive on the crime itself he has not a single crime-scene picture, not one having any evidentiary value. He decided that baby pictures of Oswald and of others already widely published of Oswald in Minsk were more important. Pictures of evidence were less to his liking. It is his book; he has his rights, and so do others, to question and to interpret.

While Studebaker is a nonperson to Posner, his boss, Lieutenant Carl Day, appears on six pages of this chapter without Posner mentioning him in connection with the finding of that rifle. He also took pictures of it as did Studebaker. And testified to its finding.

All the evidence is that Posner wrote what he knew is untrue on Oswald's alleged getting rid of that rifle. Posner's words, are that "Oswald dropped the rifle into an opening between several large boxes."

Posner's knowingly false representation of this is essential in his phony time reconstruction of Oswald's alleged flight, but it has another, considerable importance. It is actually proof that Oswald did not and could not have put the rifle where it was found and, if in flight, he could not possibly have put it there *as it was found*. It is the reason Posner does not mention those pictures.

Later, when Posner gets to the finding of the rifle, about which he had already conditioned his reader's mind, he lets slip the fact that it was "hidden." This is in the part of a single paragraph (on page 271) that he devotes, knowingly inadequately and incompletely, to the finding of the rifle.

He knows that Oswald could not just have "dropped" the rifle (page 264) while allegedly rushing to escape and by "dropping" it also have "hidden" it as he lets slip out seven pages later.

Like all his dishonesties, this is not without purpose. It is essential to his knowingly false time reconstruction that in turn is indispensable to the possibility of his having the book he ended up with.

This is his entire account of the finding of the rifle: "Ten minutes after the shells were found, Deputy Sheriff Eugene Boone and Deputy Constable Seymour Weitzman were near the northwest corner of the sixth floor when they spotted the rifle, hidden between boxes only three feet from the rear stairwell. No one touched it until Lt. Day arrived. Day could immediately estimate the chances for recovery of prints, and it was poor. 'I looked down between the boxes and saw the rifle had a well-worn leather strap. I knew there could be no fingerprints on that strap, so I picked the gun up by that. The stock was pretty porous and weather-worn, so there was little chance of any prints there. Before pulling the bolt, an alive round fell out. There were no more shells in the magazine.' " 27 (Page 271.)

His source note is his own "Interview with Carl Day." (Page 546.)

This, as will be apparent, strongly suggests that at the least some of Posner's boasted-of two hundred interviews had the purpose of giving him a source for knowingly deceptive, misleading, and just plain false writing with which he builds his phony case.

Lieutenant Day did testify before the Commission (4H249ff) and he also filed an affidavit for the record (7H401). All that Posner attributes to him through his interview was in the Commission's record. Thus no Day interview was required for Posner to obtain the information he already had in the Commission's volumes.

Setting forth the deliberateness of this particular dishonesty vital to his book, there is what he knew from *Whitewash* about the finding of the rifle. This also tells us something about the quality, or lack of it, in police terms, of the work the police did. The identification experts are Day and his assistant, Detective Studebaker. The time is after the empty shells were found:

> By this time what happened when the identification experts were called over to where the rifle had been found should be comprehensible in a streamlined account. There is no indication the area was checked for fingerprints at all, even though the rifle was completely surrounded by boxes and carefully hidden in a space 'just wide enough to accommodate that rifle and hold it in an upright position' (4H259). By 'upright,' Day meant horizontal. He and Studebaker clambered all over the unfingerprinted barriers behind which the rifle was hidden to take pictures, but they took only similar pictures from exactly the same spot. Studebaker's even show his own knee as he photographed downward (21H645).
>
> After the rifle was photographed, Day held it by the stock. He assumed the stock would show no prints. Then Captain Fritz, perhaps because of the presence of newsmen, grasped the bolt and ejected a live cartridge. Day had found no fingerprints on the bolt. If there was any need for this operation, it was never indicated. There was no print on either the clip or the live bullet.
>
> As with all the evidence, the pictures of the rifle also have other minor mysteries. Day testified that he made a negative

(Exhibit 514) from one of his two negatives (Exhibit 718) of the rifle in the position in which it was found. What useful purpose this served, especially if the result sought was greater clarity, is not apparent (4H257ff). If these are identical, they were at the very least cropped differently. The confusion extended to the commission's editor, who described the copied negative as 'Depicting location of the C2766 rifle when discovered' but of the original negative said, 'Photograph of rifle hidden beneath boxes . . .'

In any event, the rifle was almost clean of prints, as were the shells, and well hidden. Two men appear to have found it at the same time. The commission saw fit to call only one to Washington. He is Eugene Boone, a deputy sheriff (3H291ff). The other was Seymour Weitzman, a constable and one of the rare college graduates in the various police agencies. He had a degree in engineering. Weitzman gave a deposition to the Commission staff in Dallas on April 1, 1964 (7H105–9). Under questioning, he described 'three distinct shots,' with the second and third seeming almost simultaneous. He heard some one say the shots 'came from the wall' west of the Depository and 'I immediately scaled that wall.' He and the police and 'Secret Service as well' noticed 'numerous kinds of footprints that did not make sense because they were going in different directions.' This testimony seems to have been ignored. He also turned a piece of the President's skull over to the Secret Service. He got it after being told by a railroad employee that 'he thought he saw somebody throw something through a bush.'

Then he went to the sixth floor where he worked with Boone on the search. With Weitzman on the floor under the flats of boxes and Boone looking over the top, they found the rifle, 'I would say simultaneously. . . . It was covered with boxes. It was well protected . . . I would say eight or nine of us stumbled over that gun a couple of times . . . We made a man-tight barricade until the crime lab came up. . . .' " (7H106–7) (quoted from *Whitewash* pages 35–6)

(Aside from its intended purpose, exposing the true character of the massive disinformation campaign of which Posner was the point man and times to coincide with the thirtieth assassination anniversary, these quotations are of and are based upon the official evidence little known today. The no-conspiracy theory books like Posner's and those espousing conspiracy theories on the other side argue preconceptions in which the basic and established fact of the assassination and its investigation are not used. It is evidence universally ignored yet is essential to full reader understanding.)

Constable Weitzman's is only some of the testimony that ruins Posner's book. He omitted this testimony, of which he knew from more than this publication of it. His intent is to hide, as is his initial description of how Oswald allegedly got rid of that rifle.

In this paragraph quoted above he says that Deputy Sheriff Eugene Boone and Weitzman found the rifle. His source on that sentence, after his use of "they" to refer to both, is the testimony Homicide Captain Will Fritz, and that of Luke Mooney, another deputy sheriff, neither of whom had firsthand information. No mention of Weitzman or Boone or to their testimonies (page 546) or to Day's, as we see soon. Citing Weitzman's or Boone's testimony would direct readers' attention to it, and Posner does not want his readers to know the truth he suppressed from his book.

And that truth is that the rifle he said was merely "dropped" casually was in fact hidden so completely that Weitzman decided that this description just quoted fell short of how completely it was hidden. As we resume quotation of what Posner knew from *Whitewash*—and the uncritical media would have known—with what Weitzman testified to, he said it was better hidden than the police pictures that Posner also keeps secret reflect:

> When shown three unidentified photographs that seem to be those the police took, Weitzman said of the one with the hidden rifle, 'it was more hidden than there' (7H108). If it had not been so securely hidden, he said, 'we couldn't help but see it' from the stairway (Ibid). In addition to his

only too graphic testimony about the finding and hiding of
the rifle, Weitzman provided information about seemingly
meaningful footprints at a place not in conformity with
the official theories of the crime and about a strange effort
to hide a piece of the President's skull. All this should
have been valuable information for the members of the
Commission. Why he was not called to appear before the
full Commission is a mystery. Boone, who *was* called, did
not have such testimony to offer.

Weitzman's testimony about the care and success with
which the rifle was hidden and about the searchers stumbling over it without finding it is important in any time
reconstruction. With the almost total absence of fingerprints on a rifle that took and held prints and the absence
of prints on the clip and shells that would take prints, this
shows the care and time taken by the alleged user of the
weapon. That this version is not in the Report can be
understood best by comparison with the version that is."
(*Whitewash*, page 36)

In interviewing Day, Posner eliminated any need to cite
Day's testimony. But he did testify as Weitzman and Boone
did. When Day was asked if the rifle had been moved before
he photographed it he evaded direct answer, perhaps because
he did not know. But Weitzman did testify that when he found
it the rifle was "more hidden" than in the picture. The picture
I published in *Whitewash* on page 211 is in the Commission's
volumes. Posner could not have missed it.

This is the exact opposite of what Posner says, based on his
interview of Day, quoted above. He also knew what the picture
shows in *Whitewash*. It is not necessary to quote all of Day's
testimony (4H257–8). Exhibit 514 (17H224) actually proves
Weitzman's points that the police kept peeling the covering
from that rifle. And before it was all over, asked again on the
next page if the rifle had been "removed," Day responded, "I
do not remember."

Mr. Day: I met Captain Fritz. He wanted photographs of the rifle before it was moved.

Mr. Belin: Do you remember if Captain Fritz told you that the rifle had not been moved?

Mr. Day: He told me he wanted photographs before it was moved, if I remember correctly. He definitely told me it had not been moved, and the reason for the photographs he wanted it photographed before it was moved.

Mr. Belin: I am going to hand you what the reporter has marked or what has been marked as Commission Exhibit 718, and ask you to state, if you know, what this is.

Mr. Day: It is a picture of the portion of the northwest floor where the rifle was found. This is a distance shot showing the stack of boxes.

Mr. Belin: Is Commission Exhibit 718 a print from the same negative as Commission Exhibit 514?

Mr. Day: The same negative?

Mr. Belin: Yes, sir.

Mr. Day: No, I don't think so. This is a copy of this picture.

Mr. Belin: You are saying 514 was made, I assume, as a copy of 718. By that you mean a negative, a second negative, was made of 718 from which 514 was taken?

Mr. Day: Yes, sir.

Mr. Belin: Otherwise it is the same?

Mr. Day: Yes, sir.

Mr. Belin: 718 appears to be a little clearer and sharper.

Mr. Day: You can tell from looking at the two pictures which is the copy.

Mr. Belin: Was any other picture of that rifle made in that position?

Mr. Day: Nos. 22 and 23 were both made.

Mr. Belin: Your pictures which you have marked No. 22 and No. 23 were both made, one was made by you, is that Commission Exhibit 718—

Mr. Day: Yes, sir.

Mr. Belin: And the other was made by—

Mr. Day: Detective Studebaker.

Mr. Belin: Whose knee appears?

Mr. Day: Yes, sir; showing. Identical shots, we just made both to be sure that one of us made it, and it would be in focus.

Mr. Belin: For this reason I am introducing only 718, if that is satisfactory.

Mr. McCloy: Very well.

Mr. Belin: How did you stand to take the picture, Exhibit 718?

Mr. Day: I was on top of a stack of boxes to the south of where the gun was found.

Even after the protective covering had been partly removed it is apparent that placing the rifle as it was found took some care and time, should have left fingerprints, which it did not, and none of the considerable amount of time this alone took is included in any time reconstruction, notoriously not in Posner's contrived one.

When a writer can be this thoroughly dishonest when writing about that most subversive of crimes, the assassination of a President, his word cannot be taken for anything at all.

It is beyond belief that anyone could do this for money and for the attention a diligent and competent publisher could and did get him, and then say all he said on all those radio and TV shows. But it is too early to ask, "can anyone be more dishonest?"

Dishonestly as the Commission also handled the supposed reenactment of Oswald's alleged departure from the sixth floor, with regard to these pictures Day took the table of contents for the volume says of the picture, Exhibit 718 that it is a "photograph of the rifle hidden *beneath* boxes. . . ." (Emphasis added.) There Exhibit 719 is described as "showing the boxes behind which the rifle was concealed." (17H xvii)

In an effort made futile by Marrion Baker's own sworn testimony is Posner's customary No-Source mode for mininformation. Posner had earlier in his skipping around tried to make a case that it would have taken Baker much longer to get to where he saw Oswald than even the Commission says it did. That was in the second-floor room that had pop-dispensing ma-

chines in it. Nobody had a more urgent need to make it appear
that Baker took more time than the Commission said for its
story to have any credibility at all. Oswald has to have time to
get inside that employees' room, the automatic door closure has
to have closed the door slowly, and then Oswald has to have
had time to go to the Coke machine all before Baker saw him.
The Commission could not make it work out, even with incredible shortcuts, and it again merely concluded contrary to all its
own evidence, that the impossible was possible. Posner winds
up almost two pages on this matter (2264–5) with this footnote:

> Baker claimed he encountered Oswald less than two
> minutes after the assassination, and for some it is difficult to
> imagine how Oswald could have crossed the sixth floor and
> been on the second, not out of breath, in such a short time.
> The Warren Commission did a reconstruction. Officer Baker
> recreated Oswald's actions (including hiding the rifle) and in
> two tests made it to the second-floor lunch room, in "normal
> walking," in 1 minute and 18 seconds, and in a "fast walk"
> in 1 minute and 14 seconds (WC Vol. III, p. 254). A Secret
> Service agent, John Howlett, also completed Oswald's route
> in the necessary time. Neither Baker nor Howlett was out of
> breath when he reached the spot where Oswald had been
> stopped (WC Vol. VII, p. 592).

It pays to check Posner out. What he cites is a very short,
conclusory affidavit in which Secret Service Agent John Howlett does say at the end, "I was not short-winded." But what
else he says, and does not say, is again utterly destructive of
Posner's made-up case.

Posner's argument and indeed, the path shown in his Appendix A (pages 480, unnumbered, and 481) is a direct, straight-
line path for Oswald from that southeasternmost window to the
northwest corner of that sixth floor. That, of course, speeded
the imaginary Oswald up considerably. But as Posner certainly
knew, that warehouse floor was pretty solid with stacks of car-
toned books. Howlett could not take the path Posner pretends
and his appendix shows because of all those stacks of books.

Howlett's own account of what he had to do is, that he went "northerly along the east aisle to the northeast corner, then westerly along the north wall past the elevators to the northwest corner. There I placed the rifle on the floor."

He not only could not take the shortcut in his appendix that Posner knew quite well was impossible. He also did not go across that barricade of books to deposit the rifle as it was deposited. That took time and care. He also did not take the time to conceal the rifle by putting it "under" boxes and hiding the whole thing with both boxes and paper.

If what first the Commission and now Posner says Oswald did in fleeing his supposed sniper's nest does not work, as in the reconstructions it did not, then the crime is unsolved and Oswald is acquitted. It also means Posner has no book and all that meant to him. The Commission was willing to and did pull a few shortcuts in "reconstructing" Oswald's time to try to make it work out. It did not stop there. As the story is reported truthfully in *Whitewash* (pages 36–7):

Marrion L. Baker is a Dallas motorcycle policeman who heard the shots and dashed to the building, pushing people out of the way as he ran. He is the policeman who put his pistol in Oswald's stomach in the dramatic lunchroom meeting. The Commission also used him in a time reconstruction intended to show that Oswald could have left the sixth floor and been in the lunchroom in time to qualify as the assassin (3H241–70). The interrogator was Assistant Counsel David W. Belin. As so often happened, despite his understanding of his role as a prosecution witness, Baker interjected information the Commission found inconsistent with its theory. It is ignored in the Report.

The time it would have taken Oswald to get from the sixth-floor window to the lunchroom was clocked twice (3H253–4). Secret Service Agent John Joe Howlett disposed of the rifle during the reconstructions. What he did is described as 'putting' it away or, in Belin's words, he 'went over to these books and leaned over as if he were putting a rifle there?' Baker agreed to this description. But this is hardly a representation of the manner in which the rifle had been so carefully hidden. With a stopwatch and with the Howlett streamlining, they made two trips. The first one 'with normal walking took us a minute and 18 seconds . . . And the second time we did it at a fast walk which took us a minute and 14 seconds.' During this time Oswald had to clean and hide the rifle and go down to the lunchroom and 20 feet inside of it, and a door with an automatic closure had to shut. This was an additional time-consuming factor ignored in the reconstruction and the Report.

On the other hand, the first reconstruction of the time the Commission staff alleged it took Baker was actually done at a walk! In Baker's words, 'From the time I got off the motorcycle we walked the first time and we kind of ran the second time from the motorcycle on into the building.' Once they got into the building, 'we did it at kind of a trot, I would say, it wasn't a real fast run, an open run. It was more of a trot, kind of.' " (3H253).

Is there any wonder Howlett was not "short winded"?

Imagine an assassin just sauntering off to hide his weapon! They *walked a "simulation" to make it work and it still did not work, did not get Oswald to that lunchroom until after Baker was there,* and he walked to and into the building in that simulation rather than running as fast as he could.

They could not make it work even when there was no effort made to hide the rifle as it had been so effectively and carefully hidden it had not been detected the many times that space was examined, as we have seen. "Walking through a reconstruction was pure fakery and the "kind of run" or "kind of trot" was not much better. Both Baker and Roy Truly, who accompanied him once inside the building, described what would have been expected under the circumstances, a mad dash. They were running so fast that when they came to a swinging office door on the first floor it jammed for a second. In actuality, Baker had sent people careening as he rushed into the building. He had been certain this building was connected with the shooting that he had immediately identified as rifle fire (3H247). The totally invalid walking reconstruction took a minute and 30 seconds. The "kind of trot" one took a minute and 15 seconds.

The reconstruction of Baker's time began at the wrong place, to help the Commission just a little more. To compare with the rifleman's timing, this reconstruction had to begin after the last shot was fired. Witnesses the Report quotes at length describe the leisureliness with which the assassin withdrew his rifle from the window and looked for a moment as though to assure himself of his success. Not allowing for his leisureliness, the assassin still had to fire all three shots before he could leave the window. Commissioner Dulles mistakenly assumed the Commission's reconstruction was faithful to this necessity. He asked Baker, 'will you say what time to what time, from the last shot?'

The nonplused Baker simply repeated, 'From the last shot.' Belin corrected them both, interjecting, 'The first shot' (3H252). Dulles asked, 'The first shot?' and was then reassured by Baker, 'The first shot.' The minimum time of the span of the shots was established by the Commission as 4.8 seconds. Hence, that much as a minimum must be added to the Baker timing. During this time, according to Baker, he had 'revved up' his motorcycle and was certainly driving it at something faster than a walk or 'kind of trot.'

Added to this impossibility are a number of improbables. Roy Truly was running up the stairs ahead of Baker and saw nothing. He retreated from a position between the second and third floors when he realized Baker was not following him. Neither he nor Baker saw the door closing, as it did, automatically. The door itself had only a tiny window, made smaller by the 45-degree angle at which it was mounted from the lunchroom. Baker saw 20 feet through this, according to his testimony. (*Whitewash*, page 37)."

When it was apparent that this reconstruction proved Oswald was not the assassin rather than that he could have been:

(Commissioner Allen) Dulles was troubled by this testimony. He asked Baker, 'Could I ask you one question . . . think carefully.' He wanted to know if Oswald's alleged course down from the sixth floor into the lunchroom apparently could have led to nowhere but the lunchroom. Baker's affirmative reply was based upon his opinion that a hallway from which Oswald could also have entered the lunchroom without using the door through which Baker said he saw him was a place where Oswald 'had no business' (3H256). This hallway, in fact, leads to the first floor, as Commission Exhibit 497 (17H212) shows. It is the only way Oswald could have gotten into the lunchroom without Truly and Baker seeing the mechanically closed door in motion. It also put Oswald in the only position in which he could have been visible to Baker through the small glass in the door. And Oswald told the police he had, in fact, come up from the first floor.

The plain and simple truth is that there is only one way Oswald could have been in that lunchroom *before* Baker and without Truly seeing him as Truly rushed up the stairs ahead of Baker. That one way, *from the Commission's own evidence, from the official* not the Posnerized "evidence," is from the first floor!

Where he had been seen!

This is why, as I brought to light in *Photographic Whitewash* (pages 210–1) in early 1967, the Commission's own files reveal the proof that Mrs. R. E. (Carolyn) Arnold told the FBI that she had seen Oswald on the first floor that day *at* 12:25 P.M.!

Aware of the import, when the FBI interviewed her on November 26, four days after the assassination, it mistimed what she said, stating incorrectly that it was "a few minutes before 12:15 P.M." that she saw Oswald.

When in March, 1964, the Commission asked the FBI to interview all employees in that building and ask them to respond to five Commission questions, Mrs. Arnold stated the time was "at about 12:25 P.M."

In taking those March statements the FBI agents who asked the questions wrote out in longhand on yellow pads what they then asked the witnesses to sign. Still acutely aware of the meaning of what Mrs. Arnold said, that she saw Oswald on that first floor, "between the front door and the double doors to the warehouse," in the handwritten statement the FBI then asked her to sign it again misstated the time. That statement set the time she gave incorrectly still again, placing it at "12:25 A.M."! She corrected that in her own handwriting.

The FBI then typed these handwritten statements for the Commission. In even its typed form, in facsimile on page 211 of that third of my books, it is apparent that the time was changed from A.M. to P.M. The "P.M." is the only typing on that full page that is out of line. It is considerably above the line, as happened with the typewriters of those days when what is typed is removed and then placed back in the typewriter.

There just was no other way, from the official evidence itself, not all of which is cited here, that Oswald could have been inside that lunchroom not seen by Truly and seen after the door had closed by Baker than coming from the first floor.

This means, as all the other *official* and officially misrepresented evidence also means, that Oswald could not have been in that sixth-floor window at the time of the assassination.

That, of course, means he was not an assassin.

And that destroys the entire official "solution" to the crime.

In turn, that is why the Commission had to hoke up an impossible "reconstruction."

There are ten references in the Report to this reconstruction. Two are specific. All conclude the reconstruction proves that Oswald could have been in the lunchroom before Baker got there and infer that he could have come from no other place than the sixth floor. The first one (R152–3) says, "The time actually required for Baker and Truly to reach the second floor on November 22 was probably longer than in the test runs." The second says, "Tests of all of Oswald's movements establish that these movements could have been accomplished in the time available to him." (R649).

Exactly the opposite is the truth. Ignoring the flummery

in these reconstructions and the obvious errors, the Commission itself proved that the unhurried assassin would have required a minute and 14 seconds. And the policeman at a "kind of trot" rather than a fast run would have required only a minute and 15 seconds less than the time-span of the shots, or at least four seconds less time. If things happened as the Report alleges, Baker would have been at the lunchroom before Oswald. And with Baker's gun in his belly, Oswald, having just killed the President, was "calm and collected" (3H252.) (Pages 37–8.)

Dulles hit the pay dirt he did not want, that the only way Oswald could have gotten to the lunchroom before Baker and Truly was by coming up from the first floor, the way the sixth-grade dropout Baker said he "had no business." And this is why Posner had to do as he did with Carolyn Arnold and with what she actually said and told the FBI rather than the various revisions of and changes in it. But that meant Oswald was not the assassin so that was unacceptable.

Whitewash's final reference to what Baker volunteered ends the fiction that Oswald then was seeking to escape. The imagined means was not possible:

> In following his role as a prosecution-type witness, Baker said that in going into the lunchroom Oswald was seeking escape. 'There is a door out here,' he alleged, 'that you can get out and to the other parts of the building.' This door leads to the conference room. The next witness in the Commission's reconstruction proved it was normally locked and, specifically, was locked that day. (Page 38)

Posner used Mrs. Robert Reid to say that although Oswald seemed calm she found his mumbled response when she said the President had been shot to be "strange." She could not make out what he said (page 266). She presented more problems with the Oswald alleged escape reconstruction, and her testimony indicates that the Commission was phonying up the time:

Getting Oswald to wherever he had to be to make the Commission's reconstruction possible was a never-ending problem. In not a single case did the time reconstructions prove the Commission right. Following the fatal Baker reconstruction was one intended to get Oswald out of the building in time. This was attempted with Mrs. Robert A. Reid. Mrs. Reid's reconstructed time from her view of the motorcade outside to her desk was fixed at two minutes. When she began to protest that it was longer, she was interrupted and diverted. Her desk was near the lunchroom and she recalled seeing Oswald walk past it, something not confirmed by other employees present. The Report thus theorizes that, whereas it took Mrs. Reid two minutes to run to her desk from the outside, Oswald could have calmly walked it in one minute. But Mrs. Reid shattered the reconstruction by undeviatingly insisting that at the time she saw Oswald he was wearing no shirt over his T-shirt. All who saw Oswald thereafter without exception say he was wearing a shirt. The Report allows no time in its departure reconstruction for Oswald to have gotten his shirt from elsewhere in the building.'' (Page 38.)

What then is the actual evidence, not Posner's fabrication, and what does it show and mean?

The actual official evidence is that Oswald did not and could not have carried a rifle into the building that morning. That the blanket in which it had allegedly been stored and the handmade paper bag in which he allegedly carried the rifle to the building did not have any oil on them from the "welled-oiled" rifle.

That he could not have been in that so-called ''sniper's nest'' at the time the shots were fired.

And on this limited basis, from the actual official evidence only, could not have been that sixth-floor assassin.

Posner had cast Howard Brennan in the role of the best of possible, but not the only, eyewitness who allegedly identified Oswald in that window. (Pages 247–50.) He did this in violent opposition to his own stated, if not often adhered to credo that ''Testimony closer to the event must be given greater weight'' (page 235). Posner preferred the ghosted book for which Brennan had precisely the interest Posner cautioned against, that witnesses could over the years be influenced. Brennan's ghosted book appeared in 1988, twenty-five years after the event, and of course he did not write that book. Posner just loved it.

In part to continue the narrative most readers today are not familiar with so they can be informed of the official as distinguished from the Posner and other versions and in part to provide still another means of evaluating Posner and his book, I continue with what that earliest of all the books had no trouble finding and reporting, the official evidence, with special attention to Brennan. He, despite all the double-talk, was the closest thing there was to an actual eyewitness of Oswald in that window. That Brennan certainly was not. I emphasize that there is no conspiracy or any other theorizing in it, as there is not in any of my books. I state also that in all the years since I wrote that factual account of the Commission's own evidence and no error has been shown in any of it, including by the Commission staff, their sycophants, or now by Posner. His dirty trick is to lump all who do not agree with the official story as I do not and never have, and thus he misleads the reader because my published work, published before he got the itch for those dirty pieces of silver and fame, proved his book to be wrong, to be a knowing fraud. So, in repeating this factual account of what that official evidence really is and said, a time-tested account, in addition to giving this official fact to the reader there is a means of comparing what Posner got so famous over with the reality that is not in his book:

The Report has no witnesses to Oswald's presumed trip from the sixth to the second floor. But the Commission had witnesses who gave evidence proving it impossible. Jack Dougherty was working on the fifth floor at the stairway where both elevators were then located. He saw no one going down the stairs. Three employees were at the windows on the fifth floor underneath the one from which the Report says the shots were fired. They testified they heard the empty cartridge cases hit the floor and the slight clicking of the operation of the rifle bolt. But all agreed that even after the shooting, when they were alerted and in some fear, they heard no one moving around on the sixth floor (3H181). Nothing but silent (3H179). Ten minutes before the shooting, Bonnie Ray Williams, one of the trio, had eaten his lunch next to this sixth floor window (3H173). Asked '. . . did you hear anything that made you feel that there was anybody else on the sixth floor with you?,' he explained, 'That is one of the reasons I left—because it was so quiet' (3H178).

Placing Oswald at that sixth-floor window was one of the most unsuccessful tasks of the Report. They had the testimony of but a single man, Howard Leslie Brennan. Congressman Gerald R. Ford, Commission member, was to describe Brennan as the most important of the witnesses in an article in *Life* dated October 2, 1964. Brennan had already described himself as a liar when lying served his purposes, as his own words will show. The Report had a section mislabeled 'Eyewitness Identification of Assassin' (R143–9).

This section begins with a prime example of the use of words to convey meaning that is the opposite of the truth. It says, 'Brennan also testified that Lee Harvey Oswald, whom he viewed in a police lineup the night of the assassination, was the man he saw fire the shots from the sixth-floor window of the Depository Building.' It is true that Brennan 'viewed' the lineup, although he appears to be the one person of whose presence the police have no written record. But he did not identify Oswald. Two pages later the Report, in its own way, acknowledges this by admitting 'he declined to make a *positive* identification of Oswald when he *first* saw him in the police lineup.' The fact is that Brennan *at no time at the lineup made any identification* (3H147–8). The next sentence reads, 'The Commission, therefore, does not base its conclusions concerning the identify of the assassin on Brennan's subsequent certain identification . . .' How certain Brennan could be of anything he saw or alleged he saw his own testimony will reflect better than any description. But the fact is that the Commission had and quoted no other so-called eyewitness.

In the balance of this section it refers to the testimony of a number of people, none of whom identified Oswald. Congressman Ford's article stated without semantics or equivocation that Brennan 'is the only known person who actually saw Lee Harvey Oswald fire his rifle at President Kennedy.' Nobody did, as Brennan admitted.

The Report imparts a new meaning to words in saying "the record indicates that Brennan was an accurate observer . . ." (R145). It says his description "most probably" led to the description broadcast by the police (R144), having forgotten its earlier and contradictory version that this broadcast was based primarily on Brennan's observations (R5). The earlier version also concedes Brennan was the "one eyewitness." Between the 12:45 police broadcast and Brennan's statement to the police the same day, there were changes in Brennan's description, but the Report calls the two descriptions "similar." The Report quotes the police broadcast of the suspect as "white, slender, weighing about 165 pounds, about 5'10" tall, and in his early thirties." Of his account to the police, the Report says "he gave the weight as between 165 and 175 pounds and the height was omitted." This information is footnoted. The source referred to in the footnote contains no description of any kind. It does not even refer to Brennan.

However, in a statement made to the Sheriff's Department immediately after the assassination (19H470), Brennan swore he saw 'a white man in his early 30's, slender and would weigh about 165–175 pounds. He had on light colored clothing but definitely not a suit.' The three different contradictory versions of the same police radio log are discussed elsewhere. The Report here refers to but two. The description given by all three included 'reported to be armed with what is believed to be a .30 caliber rifle.' The logs reveal 'no clothing description'; Brennan had one available for his statement at the sheriff's office, which was actually at the scene of the assassination.

How the Report can be vague about the source of the police description or accept the inability of the police to provide their source when there was but a single eyewitness is simply beyond comprehension. This is one of the most basic elements of both the investigation and reconstructions and cannot possibly be accepted unless unequivocally stated in the most positive terms.

A page after beginning its account of the observation of its 'accurate observer,' the Report begins apologizing for him. It says, 'although Brennan testified that the man in the window was standing when he fired the shots, most probably he was sitting or kneeling.' It does not say how Brennan would have known the height, weight and clothing of a man sitting or kneeling behind a solid 16-inch wall. Exhibit 1312, previously referred to, shows a sitting man could not have performed this feat without major contortions, and his face would have been against a double thickness of dirty windows from which the sun was reflecting. Exhibit 1311 (22H484) shows a standing man also would have had to fire through the double window.

How accurate an observer does Brennan show himself to be when under oath? He was questioned about his observation of the Negro employees he saw on the fifth floor. He was shown a photograph of the south side of the building. By accident or design it was rigged to make identification of the windows in which these Negroes had been as automatic as possible. Of the 84 windows in the picture, only four were open. One was at the western end of the building. So, in the entire side of the building in which these men had been, the only windows open just happened to be the same as those in which they actually had been, one at each, at the moment of the assassination. These were three of the four easternmost windows on the fifth floor. Of this series of adjoining windows, the only wrong window was closed.

When shown the picture, Brennan at first said he was confused. The questioning lawyer, with a big fat hint, asked if this was because some of the windows were open. It was not, and Brennan proceeded with his marking. First, he encircled two adjoining windows on the sixth floor as the one from which the assassin had fired. This was wrong, and only one had been open. Then he marked the one wrong window on the floor below as the one in which all the Negroes had been. Brennan's powers as an 'accurate observer' are preserved on page 62 of the Report, Exhibit 477. Although he had spectacularly upset the law of averages with his fifth-floor identification and had the assassin shooting out of two windows instead of one, the explanation of this photograph reads: '. . . marked by Brennan to show the window (A) in which he saw a man with a rifle, and the window (B) on the fifth floor in which he saw people watching the motorcade.'

"His testimony about what he saw cannot in any way be explained by the apology in the Report. He testified . . ."

Mr. Brennan: Well, as it appeared to me he was standing up and resting against the left window sill, with gun shouldered to his right shoulder, holding the gun with his left hand and taking positive aim and fired his last shot. As I calculate a couple of seconds. He drew the gun back from the window as though he was drawing it back to his side and maybe paused for another second as though to assure himself that he hit his mark, and then he disappeared. And, at the same moment, I was diving off of that firewall and to the right for bullet protection of this stone wall that is a little higher on the Houston side.

Mr. Belin: Well, let me ask you. What kind of a gun did you see in that window?

Mr. Brennan: I am not an expert on guns. It was, as I could observe, some type of a high-powered rifle.

Mr. Belin: Could you tell whether or not it had any kind of a scope on it?

Mr. Brennan: I did not observe a scope.

Mr. Belin: Could you tell whether or not it had one? Do you know whether it did or not, or could you observe that it definitely did or definitely did not, or don't you know?

Mr. Brennan: I do not know if it had a scope or not.

Mr. Belin: I believe you said you thought the man was standing. What do you believe was the position of the people on the fifth floor that you saw—standing or sitting?

Mr. Brennan: I thought they were standing with their elbows on the window sill leaning out.

Mr. Belin: At the time you saw this man on the sixth floor, how much of the man could you see?

Mr. Brennan: Well, I could see—at one time he came to the window and he sat sideways on the windowsill. That was previous to President Kennedy getting there. And I could see practically his whole body, from his hips up. But at the time that he was firing the gun, a possibility from his belt up.

Mr. Belin: How much of the gun do you believe that you saw?

Mr. Brennan: I calculate 70 to 85 percent of the gun. (3H144)

The men he saw "standing" on the fifth floor were kneeling behind a foot-high windowsill!

After giving his statement Brennan went home, getting there about a quarter of an hour either side of 2:45 P.M. and saw Oswald's picture 'twice on television before I went down to the police station for the lineup.' At the lineup he failed to identify Oswald. He admitted to the Commission that he later told a different story to a federal investigator. This is Brennan's explanation:''

Mr. Brennan: Well, he asked me—he said, "You said you couldn't make a positive identification." He said, "Did you do that for security reasons personally, or couldn't you?" And I told him I could with all honesty, but I did it more or less for security reasons—my family and myself.

Mr. Belin: What do you mean by security reasons for your family and yourself?

Mr. Brennan: I believed at that time, and still believe, it was a Communist activity, and I felt like there hadn't been more than one eyewitness, and if it got to be a

known fact that I was an eyewitness, my family or I,
either one, might not be safe.

Mr. Belin: Well, if you wouldn't have identified him,
might he not have been released by the police?

Mr. Brennan: Beg pardon?

Mr. Belin: If you would not have identified that man positively, might he not have been released by the police?

Mr. Brennan: No. That had been a great contributing factor—greater contributing factor than my personal reasons was that I already knew they had the man for
murder, and I knew he would not be released.

Mr. Belin: The murder of whom?

Mr. Brennan: Of Officer Tippit.

Mr. Belin: Well, what happened in between to change your
mind that you later decided to come forth and tell them
you could identify him?

Mr. Brennan: After Oswald was killed, I was relieved
quite a bit that as far as pressure on myself of somebody
not wanting me to identify anybody, there was no longer
that immediate danger.

Mr. Belin: What is the fact as to whether or not your
having seen Oswald on television would have affected
your identification of him one way or the other?

Mr. Brennan: That is something I do not know. (3H148)

"Despite the end of his fears, Brennan did not commu-
nicate with the police or federal agents following Oswald's
murder. Yet he had presumed he was the only eyewitness
(3H160). The basis for his alleged fears is melted elsewhere in the testimony, startling the examiner:"

Mr. Brennan: Well, don't you have photographs of me
talking to the Secret Service men right here?

Mr. Belin: I don't believe so.

Mr. Brennan: You should have. It was on television before
I got home—my wife saw it.

Mr. Belin: On television?

Mr. Brennan: Yes.

Mr. Belin: At this time we do not have them. Do you remember what station they were on television?

Mr. Brennan: No. But they had it. And I called I believe Mr. Lish who requested that he cut those films or get them out of the FBI. I believe you might know about them. Somebody cut those films, because a number of times later the same films were shown, and that part was cut out. (3H150)

And despite the assurance of the Report that Brennan 'saw a rifle being fired' (R5), Brennan testified to the contrary. Asked by Commission member McCloy, 'Did you see the rifle discharge, did you see the recoil or the flash?' Brennan replied, 'No.' (3H154)

Almost all of Brennan's testimony is preposterous and impossible. But of one thing there is no doubt: He spoke to the police immediately. As though it were something unusual, he testified he may have run across the street 'because I have a habit of, when something has to be done in a hurry, I run.' He reported the rifle on the sixth floor (3H145). He also incorrectly said he spoke to Secret Service Agent Sorrels at that time, but Sorrels was not there.

This was about 10 minutes before the alert was broadcast and within seconds the whole area was alive with radio-equipped police vehicles. At least one, that of Sergeant D. V. Harkness, was parked on that corner before the assassination. No explanation of the crucial delay of about 14 minutes is offered, nor was one asked for. (Pp. 38–42.)

The fact of the assassination is not in Posner's book nor was telling it his intention. The dishonesty is unending and, without this permeating dishonesty, he has no book. Whenever dishonesty is required he is up to it. Misrepresenting established fact is his forte and omitting what he knows and is true is one of the means by which he undertook to rewrite the truth about the assassination, whatever his motive or motives may be.

What he has done has among its requirements ignoring the truth.

That presented no problem to Posner.

And this is what he used all those 200 interviews for—to avoid the truth, the known fact—the actual testimony.

To rewrite our history.

To be.

And then to promote his book based on these lies.

VIII
That Dubious Epitaph

Posner pretends to get into the specifics of the medical evidence with the subchapter "The Neck Wound" (Page 304) of his "He Had a Death Look" chapter but in only one page he is already arguing against the actual evidence with such irrelevancies as quoting Dr. Malcolm Perry, who had stated at the official press conference that this neck wound was in the front as saying he did not know where from the front it came. (Page 305.)

Yes. This is still another of his interviews he conducted to rewrite our history. (Page 551)

Careful to avoid the largest and most definitive published sources of the medical evidence, my books, especially *Post Mortem*, he makes the most astounding and stupid factual errors. In his trying to argue against the established medical fact that is uncongenial to his concoction, he states that "less than 1mm of metallic dust particles was evident on the X rays of the President's head." (Page 307.) The first of his sources (page 551) actually said there were some forty such particles! This also was known from the time my 1965 book was completed and, as Posner had it more extensively in my 1975 *Post Mortem*.

135

There is nothing in this chapter worth any time and taking the time for other than to expose its lack of honest intent. Little more of that is now needed. Besides, in the next chapter it is relatively spectacular, even for the Posner we have seen to this point.

The killer chapter as it is designed to be, is titled with the supposed words of the other assassination-shooting victim, Texas Governor John B. Connally, "My God, they are going to kill us all!" That by this Connally was instinctively saying there was a conspiracy—"they" were doing the killing—was lost on Posner. He set out with the pat formulae that the fame and money were in arguing there had not been a conspiracy, whatever the evidence showed. This is his chapter of his ultimate proof. (Pages 321–342.)

Not to take it out of order but to set the tone and establish Posner's concepts of truth, accuracy, honor, ethics, and morals that we began with, a small part of this his intended killer chapter, with his pretending that he and he alone made an amazing and entirely new "discovery," the unprecedented, revolutionary discovery coming from what he, Dick Daring, saw in that amazing, unprecedented "enhancement" of the Zapruder film. That turned out to be a calculated theft from a story by a fifteen-year-old boy, David Lui. We saw also how calculated his thievery was, masking it with his tricky endnotes that characterize his unrivaled scholarship. Not realizing that he was lampooning himself in this or, the inadequacy of his scholarship being what it is, or not caring, although it is explicit in Lui's article some of which he stole, Posner's actual source, which had nothing at all to do with his rare "enhancements." was the unaided vision of that boy, who had as his source a pirated and not very clear copy of that film. Lui neither had nor needed any "enhancement." That ten years earlier the same information was available—published—with no access to that film at all—Posner masked by attributing to the Nobel Laureate Luis Alvarez what Alvarez's students had read in *Whitewash* and asked him about, that "jiggle theory." It was first reported in the same book a decade before Lui saw it.

Posner's misrepresentations had brief treatment only, on page

321. He then jiggled that on the next page with Alvarez. Treating that brazen theft earlier in this book served to inform the reader about the true nature of the book and its much-heralded author. I deemed that both were necessary and fair to prepare the reader for the unprecedented dishonesty of the entire project in its rewriting of our history before the largest possible international audience. Posner's publisher and the CIA were his indispensable partners.

Once again, what Posner does in this, his important, wrap-up chapter, reflects the absolute indispensability in responsible publishing; publishing intended to be honest and faithful to fact on controversial nonfiction, of authentic peer review. In demonstrating this all over again it is not necessary to address and assess all the dishonesties and errors in it. Posner's intended trickery and thievery with those innocent children, the ten-year-old Willis girl and the fifteen-year-old Lui boy, are faithful to this chapter and to the entire book.

This chapter alone also reflects the fact that while Posner castigates all "theories," to him theories being restricted to represent "conspiracies" only, in fact his book is dependent upon a larger number of them and a wider variety of them than any of the books espousing theorized conspiracies to kill. His book, like the Warren Report itself, is a theory, the opposite theory, that there was no conspiracy to kill.

From the time that Report was issued there was never any question about this. It is a concatenation of theories. In a few of the previous chapters we have seen how, on impartial examination, the supposed supporting evidence does not exist and, in fact, that supposed supporting evidence not only proved the opposite of what was alleged officially, it actually proves that Oswald was framed.

Only the willing collaboration of the major media in that palpably untenable official mythology kept that Report from exploding in official faces on its issuance.

Of all the many attractive targets Posner presents in this his wrap-up of the evidence chapter, the one that initially interested me most, is indispensable to his baseless fabrication, that the first of the known and admitted shots is the other that missed.

It typifies what those dust-jacket puffer-uppers describe as his research, saying that it is "brilliant" (two of the four), "meticulous," "historical," "always conclusive," and "thoroughly documented."

We assess this too, with what is Posner's absolute need for him to have a book at all, his thievery-based theory, and it is only a theory, that the first shot missed. His "proof" of the claimed timing is that the little girl stopped and looked around because she heard that shot at that moment, for all the world as though what causes a child to do anything can be determined with certainty when it is not in fact known. James T. Tague suffered a minor injury from that first shot. We now examine Posner's version of Tague's story and what he represents is the scientific evidence supporting his version.

In it Posner again demonstrates one of his major purposes in all those time-consuming and costly interviews: he uses them to avoid the official proof that does not suit his preconceptions as well as what he can contrive by ignoring that available official evidence. Voluminous and court-tested official evidence too. And all available to him free and at the very outset of his work.

This official evidence begins with Tague's Warren Commission testimony (7H552ff.). It includes all I obtained in those two FOIA lawsuits, the first of which led to amending the Act in 1974 to open FBI, CIA, and other such files to FOIA access. It includes what both sides used and produced in that litigation. It includes all the documents I obtained in that suit, C.A. 75–0226, and in the related suits, C.A.s. 78–0322 and 0420. The first was for the results of all the FBI's scientific testing and the second was for the assassination records of, first, the FBI's Dallas office and the second, those of its New Orleans office records. It includes the depositions I took of four of those FBI lab agents, and this is relevant to more of Posner's horsing around with sacred history than the Tague missed shot element in what these agents testified to under oath. It also includes an affidavit Tague, assisted by his wife Judy, prepared for me to present and I did present in that suit for the test results.

This affidavit has the merit, the value, of being an independent statement of what Tague knew and believed to be significant.

All of this plus my file of correspondence with the Tagues was right where Posner spent those three days searching and copying from my files. He never asked me a word about the Tagues, the evidence I obtained, or what those lab agents testified to or what I had learned by more effort than is required in writing a book, or what I had published, which he had and could use anyway. In three days, important, really as indispensable as all of this information is to any honest writing about it, Posner never asked me anything about it. He never indicated even casual interest in it or curiosity about it. He told me his book would not address any such information. And he wound up substituting his own January 1992 interview of Jim Tague as his sole source on what Jim Tague said and knew and could say. Posner is finished with that in a single paragraph of about a third of a page in his treatment of this missed shot of only about two pages in all. (Pages 324–6.)

What Posner used of that interview he says was over a two-day period (page 553) is less by far than was available in many published sources ranging from the newspapers to my books.

For this Posner had to go to Texas and spend two days interviewing Tague?

Again, bearing on his intentions from the outset and his lies to me about what his book would address and be limited to, his interview was the month before he came here.

This makes the dishonesty of his intent what he began with.

What Tague testified to and how he came to testify and the importance of that date is not reflected even in Posner's end notes (page 553). Posner's readers cannot tell from his book even that Tague testified before the Warren Commission, let alone participated in the lawsuit to bring the evidence as reflected in FBI records that Posner uses—without crediting his source—to light. There is no reference to that lawsuit in the book, either. All of this is really "brilliant" and "meticulous" research—but only for an intended disinformation.

I was not interested in disinformation. I was interested in information that would have been important to Posner if he had ever had the slightest interest in what those poor, deceived big-name, prepublication endorsers refer to as "historical," "brilliant," and "meticulous" research.

But even how this missed-bullet matter, which the Commission had entirely ignored, was forced upon it and what that then required of it is suppressed by Posner. He gets himself so tied up in his whitewashing that he even stumbles over his own covering up that is indispensable to his own concoction.

Tague was slightly wounded by a spray of concrete from the curbstone twenty feet east of the triple underpass struck by that missed bullet. We'll come to why the FBI had to dig it up. But the facts are so far from Posner's concern that he has the FBI digging that section of curbstone ("sample" to him), the month before it had to and did. (Page 325.)

My source on what compelled the Commission to acknowledge the existence of this missed shot, of which it and the FBI knew from the outset, was *The Dallas Morning News* then chief photographer, Tom Dillard. Although I tell the story that follows in *Post Mortem*, which Posner had, and a print of the picture of where that missed shot impacted that Dillard gave me is in that book, he is mentioned by Posner only twice, once as merely a "witness," (page 237) and then as a "journalist" (page 246) and thus Posner deliberately suppresses all that lets his reader know that Dillard was a professional photographer and took pictures of enormous evidentiary importance. We see his remaining picture later.

What Dillard told me and is completely validated by the documents I obtained in the litigation is that when in June, 1964, he covered a news event just after one of those innumerable leaks by the FBI to condition the public mind for what was coming, the account of what was as of that time the official "solution," and he saw Harold Barefoot Sanders, the Dallas United States Attorney there, he told him that the story he had seen was wrong because it did not mention that missed shot the impact of which he had photographed the day after the assassination and his paper had published. Sanders notified Rankin in writing through his assistant, Martha Joe Stroud, and as of the moment Rankin got the information from Sanders the

Commission could no longer ignore that missed shot. The farcical nature of what then ensued, not the least of it the FBI's self-portrayal as Keystone Kops, along with the background including how early the Commission knew about that missed shot, really even so much more than Posner has in his 1993 "brilliantly researched" treatment so indispensable to his entire mythology, was first public in 1965, in *Whitewash*, which Posner had, on page 158:

> Minutes after the assassination, Patrolman L. L. Hill radioed, 'I have one guy that was possibly hit by a ricochet from the bullet of the concrete' (R116). James T. Tague had left his car at the end of Dealey Plaza opposite the Depository. He was slightly injured on the cheek and immediately reported this to Deputy Sheriff Eddy R. Walthers (7H547, 553), who was already examining the area to see if any bullets had hit the turf. Patrolman J. W. Foster, on the Triple Underpass, had seen a bullet hit the turf near a manhole cover. Other witnesses in the same location made and reported similar observations. Walthers found a place on the curb near where Tague had stood where it appeared a bullet had hit the cement, in the words of the Report. According to Tague, 'There was a mark. Quite obviously, it was a bullet, and it was very fresh (R116).'
>
> Photographs of this spot were taken by two professional photographers who were subsequently witnesses in another connection. Tom Dillard had photographed the south face of the Book Depository Building. James R. Underwood, a television news director, had made motion pictures of the same area and had been in the motorcade.
>
> From its own records, the Commission did not look into this until July 7, 1964, when it asked the FBI to make an investigation, which produced nothing. I discovered this entirely by accident, for there is no logical means by which to learn of it. What follows is a credit to neither the FBI nor the Commission:
>
> "Not until September 1, with its work almost done,

did the Commission call back Lyndal Shaneyfelt, the FBI photographic, not ballistics, expert. Assistant Counsel Norman Redlich took a deposition from him beginning at 10:45 A.M. at the Commission's offices (15H–686–702).

The previous investigation was reported in an unsigned memorandum of July 17, 1964, from the Dallas field office (21H472ff). In it, the author politely called to the Commission's attention that the photographs in question 'had been forwarded to the President's Commission by Martha Joe Stroud, Assistant United States Attorney, Dallas, Texas.'

In other words, if the FBI was going to be subject to criticism for not finding what the Commission wanted, the FBI was going to have it on record that there was no need for the Commission to have delayed seeking further information.

This FBI report quoted Dillard as locating the point at which he took the picture. It was, he said, 'on the south side of Main Street about twenty feet east of the triple underpass.' The FBI Dallas office said, 'The area of the curb from this point for a distance of ten feet in either direction was carefully checked and it was ascertained that there was no nick in the curb in the checked area, nor was any mark observed.' In the concluding paragraph, repeating the above information almost word for word, the Dallas Field Office concluded, 'It should be noted that, since this mark was observed on November 23, 1963, there have been numerous rains, which could have possibly washed away such a mark and also that the area is cleaned by a street cleaning machine about once a week, which would also wash away any such mark.'

Imagine the fabled FBI telling the Commission that rain or street-cleaning equipment could "wash" solid concrete away!

There is much more on this, including the Dillard, James Underwood, and official curbstone pictures in *Post Mortem*, pages 454, 460, and 608–9. Aside from the fact that all of this does not exist to the Posner of that truly "definitive" and "historical" research and thus he does not tell his reader about it underscores the original dishonest intent of his entire project, this something-special book.

What Dillard, who was very friendly, open, and accommodating, told me is that after he informed Sanders of the actuality of the missed shot and the existing proof of it and Sanders put Stroud to work on it and the Commission finally, more than a half year too late, got cracking on it, those Dillard referred to as "the federales" came and took his best negatives of that bullet impact mark on that curbstone. I was so fascinated by his first-person account of this so-important an element in that so-important event in our history, proof that a Presidential Commission was proceeding with what it knew was an enormous fraud in its "solution" of that crime, I forgot to ask Dillard who he meant by the "federales." He did tell me that those negatives were not returned and he did make the print in this book for me from what he said is his best remaining negative.

Confirming that his best negatives were gone is the fact that the electrostatic copy he made of his picture as published at the time of the assassination is clearer than a print he made from his best remaining negative.

That Posner made no reference to what was published long before he began his personal rewriting of the history of that terrible crime speaks for itself. What was published in just these two books of which he knew makes his intent to lie about this most basic of evidence obvious as the design with which he began.

The Tagues were the most considerate of hosts and the most helpful when I was their guest for a week. It was a bit more chaotic than anyone could expect because that was the week James Earl Ray, alleged assassin of Martin Luther King, Jr., escaped from Tennessee's maximum security jail, Brushy Mountin. I had been his investigator. I conducted the investigation for the habeas corpus proceeding by means of which he got an evidentiary hearing. That was to determine whether or not he would get the trial he has never had. I had then conducted the investigation for those two weeks of hearings and, sitting at the counsel table during them, became known to the media as the case investigator. As a result, when Jimmy actually did escape from that mountain fastness, which after being there often and long I believed was close to impossible, I was the Tagues' guest and their phone stayed pretty busy with stacked-up calls from reporters all over the country.

There is no reason to believe that the Tagues were any less open, friendly, and helpful with Posner than they had been with me. There thus is no reason to believe that Jim Tague did not volunteer to him the story he told me that it is not possible not to interpret as solid proof of a conspiracy to kill JFK.

While this makes it understandable that Posner would not want that in his book, it also says that he knew his book was a fraud before he wrote a word, that he began intending to perpetuate that fraud. I tell the story in *Post Mortem* where I have many references to Tague, what he said, and what I learned from him (pages 55, 57, 62, 92, 120, 122, 268, 295–6, 306, 338, 453–5, 459–60).

Then, too, there is his excellent and informative affidavit I filed in that lawsuit. And the beginning of this mystery is amply covered in those Commission volumes whose content Posner invested so much time in mastering and then indexing them.

It simply is not possible that Posner did not know about what he suppressed. That he suppressed what he did is also in the FBI's interest. It should have been of interest to those whose trust he imposed upon. He makes no mention in his book of the FBI's predetermination that no missed shot be acknowledged. (In facsimile in *Whitewash*, pages 192–5.) (See also the formerly Top Secret January 21, 1964, executive session transcript in *Post Mortem*, pps. 475 ff.)

That mystery, as Wesley Liebeler learned when he deposed Tague, is that the curbstone was patched when Oswald could not have done it and when nobody other than a conspirator has any interest in what that curbstone patching meant.

Even the scientific opinion that this curbstone had been patched was in my file labeled "curbstone" in the "subject" files in which Posner spent most of his time when he was here.

I mince no words: Posner knew enough of this from what he got from me, if he did not see it all. It is also in the court records, in Tague's affidavit, and in several of my own, and that, too, tested as it was by the adversary system and undenied by the government, Posner ignores and suppresses.

By his own standard, in his actual record despite his prating his own best evidence standard, that "Testimony closer to the event must be given greater weight," yet he depends on his 1992 interview and ignores all better sources. When he had all that 1964 testimony free? All in that 1965 book that brought that testimony and the then available related evidence to light, and he had that?

This despite all the treatment and photographs in *Post Mortem* that he also had?

Despite all that emerged in the lawsuits that lasted a decade and filled file cabinet drawers?

This, a scant single paragraph in 600 pages, with all that he ignored at hand, and for what was no more than a brief newspaper story he took *two days to interview Jim Tague*?

There are fascinating aspects to this intriguing history, he had at the least the leads and knowledge of the probabilities, he could have had it all, and if he did not ask Tague what he knew about it, unless Tague knew he did not want it, there is no reason to believe that Tague did not volunteer it.

Or is it—can it possibly be—that not later than January 19 and 20, 1992, he knew without question that there had been a conspiracy to kill the President and he still went ahead and published this monument to his unique capabilities that says, with all that impressive endorsement and all that unprecedented international attention—the exact opposite of what he had from other sources when right there in front of him he had the best first-person source on some of it in the entire world to give him all the details?

That is investigating? A crime of this magnitude?

Well, it is, Posner-style, apparently.

If by any chance, despite his boasted-of career as a "Wall Street lawyer," he found comprehending the testimony too much for him, that same testimony of which he set out to and did present himself as the world's great authority—the testimony he even indexed—it was simplified and drawn together for him in what he had, *Post Mortem*.

There they were, just the two of them, Tague and Liebeler, plus the secret-keeping court reporter who took it all down for verbatim transcription, beginning at 3:15 P.M. the afternoon of July 23, 1964, "in the office of the United States attorney" in Dallas. (7H552–8, not a long deposition, either.) Liebeler had gone over what had appeared in the papers with Tague, that he had been wounded slightly, then how his minor wound was observed before he was aware of it, then that there was a short period in which Liebeler did not interrupt Tague. Tague then testified that the unnamed deputy with whom he walked to the spot on impact, probably the late Buddy Walthers, when the Deputy said, "Look here on the curb," and Tague then said, "There was a mark quite obviously that was a bullet and it was very fresh." (Page 443.) A policeman even said that he had seen something flying up from the curbstone. Then came the beginning of the surprise.

I use the official published transcript in which Posner had allegedly immersed himself for his massive study and indexing rather than my bringing of it all together for easier reading because Posner clearly does not approve of my books. Not that his reader can get the vaguest notion of what they are or what they contain or do. In his ten references to me he mentions only one book, the first, once because he believes I should have loved that shrink Hartog as he did, and once a general comment. But his disapproval is clear, so I use the official transcript. I quote a little more than for the point I next make because it is informative and because we return to it later as we learn more about why Posner went to all that cost and trouble for so many of those two hundred interviews he had:

Mr. Liebeler: Do you have any idea which bullet might have made that mark?

Mr. Tague: I would guess it was either the second or third. I wouldn't say definitely on which one.

Mr. Liebeler: Did you hear any more shots after you felt yourself get hit in the face?

Mr. Tague: I believe I did.

Mr. Liebeler: How many?

Mr. Tague: I believe that it was the second shot, so I heard the third shot afterwards.

Mr. Liebeler: Did you hear three shots?

Mr. Tague: I heard three shots; yes sir. And I did notice the time on the Hertz clock. It was 12:29.

Mr. Liebeler: That was about the time that you felt yourself struck?

Mr. Tague: I just glanced. I mean I just stopped, got out of my car, and here came the motorcade. I just happened upon the scene.

Mr. Liebeler: Now I understand that you went back there subsequently and took some pictures of the area, isn't that right?

Mr. Tague: Pardon?

Mr. Liebeler: I understand that you went back subsequently and took some pictures of the area.

Mr. Tague: Yes; about a month ago.

Mr. Liebeler: With a motion picture camera?

Mr. Tague: Yes; I didn't know anybody knew about that.

Mr. Liebeler: I show you Baker Exhibit No. 1, and ask you if you took that picture.

Mr. Tague: No; not to my knowledge.

Mr. Liebeler: In point of fact, that picture was taken by another individual; I confused the picture taken by somebody else with the picture I thought you had taken. You, yourself did take pictures of the area about a month ago?

Mr. Tague: Yes; my wife and I were going to Indianapolis. This is the home of my parents. I was taking some pictures of the area to show to them. This was the latter part of May.

Mr. Liebeler: Did you look at the curb at that time to see if the mark was still there?

Mr. Tague: Yes.

Mr. Liebeler: Was it still there?

Mr. Tague: Not that I could tell. (7H555–6)

Tague was surprised that Liebeler or anyone else knew that he had returned to where he became part of the country's history that fateful day to take pictures so he could show them to his parents when he went there on a planned visit. Liebeler never told him how they knew Tague had taken any or why he believed he had Tague's picture. Tague was still puzzled about that years later when I was his guest for that week.

I have seen no Commission or FBI record with any reference to any pictures Tague took. So the mystery that remains is how anyone in any official position knew of the picture and why Liebeler thought that the FBI had made prints of it for the Commission.

The big and ignored mystery is that the curbstone had been patched.

Why would anyone want to see to it that a small nick or chip or scar or hole in a curbstone was patched?

We'll come to that.

There is no greater certainty then that Lee Harvey Oswald could not have been the curbstone patcher!

Liebeler is vague about the date Tague returned to take pictures. He told me he went there with an 8-mm home movie camera and that it was in May 1964.

Then, what certainly Tague would not have kept secret from Posner after telling me about it, his home was burglarized and the only thing he could be certain had been taken was that reel of film!

The film that to the best of his knowledge nobody knew he had taken.

There were things what could have been considered of value by a burglar in Jim Tague's home. He was not, as in records officials never expected to be public they sought to deprecate him as "a used car salesman." Tague was, in fact, one of the country's highest-rated auto fleet salesman, as I recall only four in the whole country outperforming him.

But nothing else was taken.

Before we get to what else is important, because I've commented that Posner found use for only a single paragraph of those two days of his Tague interviews, examination of some of what he wrote in that third of a page can be illuminating.

He says that Tague when wounded slightly, "was standing under the southern end of the triple underpass." Tague told me, as he had testified, that he was twenty feet to the east of that, near the southern curb where Commerce, on the south, Main in the center, and Elm Street on the north funnel together to go through the underpass as a single street.

Posner says that this spot "was in a straight line from the sniper's nest." That, obviously, would be as true for any spots in a hundred-and-eighty-degree arc from that window. Dirty, dishonest writing, Posner's own, unsourced. Posner considered this deception and misrepresentation significant enough to have it two ways in that single paragraph.

Then, citing no source, Posner says that it was a bullet "fragment" that had struck the curb. If it was not, and of that there is no proof at all, on that basis alone, too, Posner has no book and there was on that basis alone a conspiracy.

So, what else *could* Posner say and still have a book?

He then quotes Tague as saying of that missed shot, "I actually can't tell you which one. I could try to pick one, but through the years I have maintained accuracy. I don't know which one hit me." (Page 325.)

Here is either a first-rate endorsement of Posner's proclaimed and ignored standard, that the testimony closer to the event is the best, because as we have already seen, "closer to the event," in his July 1964 deposition of almost thirty years before Posner's interview, Tague said—under oath—that he believed it was the second shot that missed and caused his slight injury. Obviously, Posner's book cannot survive that, either!

The Jim Tague I knew and liked impressed me as an honest man and I believed that his earned reputation for honesty is what made him as successful a vehicle fleet salesman as he was. He may have made a mistake after all those years but I do not think he did. If he did not make a mistake, then Posner was untruthful in his direct quotation of Tague. Only Posner can know.

Much of the rest of this remarkably brief treatment of what

is so vital in Posner's theory—and yes, it is all theory—is de-voted to argument, some of it the most shocking reflection of ignorance from a supposed world-class expert:

> Only a bullet fragment hit the concrete near Tague, since when the FBI later performed a spectrographic analysis on the curb, it showed 'traces of lead with a trace of antimony.' The 6.5-mm bullets used in Oswald's gun had full copper jackets (a metal covering on a bullet, designed to increase its penetration). Since there was no copper found on the curb, it meant the fragment that struck was not jacketed. Agent Lyndal Shaneyfelt testified that the lead instead came from the bullet's core. (Pages 325–6.)

Not being or claiming to be a Posnerian mind reader I freely acknowledge that there is an alternative to this representing world-class ignorance. If Posner prefers that, I have no objection.

We'll come to the actualities of that FBI spectrographic analysis that is still another vital element of Posner's no-conspiracy theory and his vaunted "solution" to the crime. The source he cites is FBI Lab Photographic Expert Lyndal L. Shaneyfelt's Commission testimony. That, by Posner's own standard as well as the standard of all, even Wall Street lawyers, still is not the best evidence. *If what Shaneyfelt actually told the Warren Commission has the meaning Posner gives it. The best evidence came from the man who did the actual testing, John F. Gallagher.* That Posner did not want. It was with all my files on that case in the stenographic transcript of our deposition of him in that case. Gallagher did know what a bullet is made of. As Posner here reveals or pretends, he, Posner, does not.

Posner's parenthetical explanation of hardened jackets on military ammunition, not the only one he gives, those he does give not being consistent either with each other or with the provisions of that Geneva international agreement on this that he does not mention, if he knows about it, that it is to "increase its penetration" is consistent with the need of Posner's fabrication. But the real reason for the jacket—and the research on this was done for me at the Pentagon by a then relatively high-ranking and very conservative friend—is to make warfare a little more "humanitarian." The jacket is to deter the bullet becoming in effect a dumdum on impact, and then to make the most horrible wounds as it tears its way through the body, spiraling more devastatingly as it goes. The jacket is to deter that, not to increase the penetration. For war this also has another value. It takes nobody out of combat to care for a corpse, but it can take the average of five men out of action to care for a wounded man. Those are five men who cannot fight the army that caused the wound.

This Posner follows with another of his absolutely necessary statements of other than fact: "Agent Shaneyfelt testified that the lead instead came from the bullet's core." (Page 326.) I do not have to check Shaneyfelt's testimony to know he did not say any such thing. And why else would No-Source Posner leave this without any source? The reason is apparent: he can have no source for that statement at all.

Before consulting what Shaneyfelt actually said and one of the remaining selections from Tague's testimony that Posner did not consider as useful as those two days of interviews he encapsulated into a single paragraph, we should bear in mind the peaens of praise we read earlier.

This is another of the endless statements that leaves but two choices in examining what Posner says. Both may apply at times. But if he knew anything at all about that kind of testimony by those kinds of experts, he would know that they never did or would make that kind of statement.

If he knew anything at all about those bullets about which he writes as though he were one of the world's most eminent experts on that basis alone he would have known that no expert could possibly make any such statement.

Even an intelligent and informed gun buff would know better.

The obvious alternative is that Posner did know and lied because he needed that lie to make his case.

We'll have more on this.

Posner's theory, and it is no more than that, so basic to the entire book, is that the first shot is the one that missed. Thus it can be understood that among the readily available sources for which he had no use is Jim Tague and his sworn Commission testimony. That, in fact, is the very close—closest—"testimony" to "the event" and thus must be "given greater weight." Only Posner's unique way of giving it "great weight" is to pretend it does not exist at all. In all those pages of his thick book it is not mentioned at all.

Liebeler was arguing with Tague about the source of the shots. In what I do not quote Tague can be said to be agreeing with him, that they all came from the TSBD building. In the beginning of this selection that Liebeler might mean by "to Tague's left" and "back" depends on what Liebeler was careful not to ask Tague, which way he was looking at the instant in question. But it soon becomes apparent that what Tague was really saying is that where those shots came from is what to Posner is the infamous Grassy Knoll. And as readers may recall, that is precisely what Zapruder told the Secret Service:

Mr. Liebeler: Immediately to your left, or toward the back? Of course, now we have other evidence that would indicate that the shots did come from the Texas School Book Depository, but see if we can disregard that and determine just what you heard when the shots were fired in the first place.

Mr. Tague: To recall everything is almost impossible. Just an impression is all I recall, is the fact that my first impression was that up by the, whatever you call the monument, or whatever it was. . . .

Mr. Liebeler: Up above No. 7?

Mr. Tague: That somebody was throwing firecrackers up there, that the police were running up there to see what was going on and this was my first impression. Somebody was causing a disturbance, that somebody had drawn a gun and was shooting at the crowd, and the police were running up to it. When I saw the people throwing themselves on the ground is when I realized

there was serious trouble, and I believe that was after
the third shot was fired.

Mr. Liebeler: Your impression of where the shots came
from was much the result of the activity near No. 7?

Mr. Tague: Not when I heard the shots.

Mr. Liebeler: You thought they had come from the area
between Nos. 7 and 5?

Mr. Tague: I believe they came from up in here.

Mr. Liebeler: Back in the area ''C''?

Mr. Tague: Right.

Mr. Liebeler: Behind the concrete monument here between
Nos. 5 and 7, toward the general area of ''C''?

Mr. Tague: Yes. (7H557)

Among Tague's identification of the Grassy Knoll as the
source of the shots is that ''the police were running up to''
where the shots came from. That is where they did run to.
Those ''concrete monuments'' were also on that knoll, well past
the westernmost end of the shed-type separate building that
itself is west of the main TSBD building from the easternmost
window of which Posner and the government say that Oswald
fired all those shots.

Back now, with those above-quoted encomiums in mind, that
that unsourced statement Posner says is what Shaneyfelt
swore to.

Because I knew that, sometimes innocently but not necessarily always, the case testimony can be altered before publication,
long before Posner, whether alone or not, saw the enormous
potential of an Oliver Stone caper from the other side, in my
own checking I went to the trouble and expense of getting the
original, unedited stenographic transcript of Shaneyfelt's Commission testimony. What follows is all of pages 43 and 44 of
that stenographic transcript except the first four words on page
43, ''. . . of the triple underpass.'' He has been testifying to his
removal of that section of curbstone to take to the FBI lab for
the FBI's most expert treatment. His description of that curbstone is as he found it that day, August 5, 1964.

What we compare this with is what Posner says that Shaneyfelt testified to, ''that the lead on the curbstone instead came from that bullet's core:

> . . . It was cut out under my supervision, and I person-
> ally returned it to the FBI laboratory. In the FBI labora-
> tory it was examined for the presence of any foreign
> material.
>
> Mr. Redlich: For the record, the results of this investiga-
> tion have been summarized in a communication from
> Director Hoover to Mr. Rankin, dated August 12, 1964,
> and designated now as the Shaneyfelt Exhibit No. 27,
> is that correct, Mr. Shaneyfelt?
>
> Mr. Shaneyfelt: That is correct.
>
> Examination of the mark on the curbing in the labora-
> tory resulted in the finding of foreign metal smears ad-
> hering to the curbing section within the area of the
> mark. These metal smears were spectographically deter-
> mined to be essentially lead with a trace of antimony.
> No copper was found.
>
> The lead could have originated from the lead core of a
> mutilated metal-jacketed bullet such as the type of bullet
> loaded into the 6.5-millimeter Mannlicher-Carcano car-
> tridges, or from some other source having the same
> composition.
>
> The absence of copper precludes the possibility that the
> mark on the curbing section was made by an unmuti-
> lated military full-metal-jacketed bullet such as the bul-
> let from Governor Connally's stretcher.
>
> The damage to the curbing would have been much more
> extensive if a rifle bullet had struck the curbing without
> first having struck some other object. Therefore, this
> mark could not have been made by the first impact of
> a high-velocity rifle bullet.
>
> Mr. Redlich: Based on your examination of the mark on
> the curb, can you tell us whether the mark which we
> have been referring to is a nick on the curb, that is, has
> a piece of the curb been chipped away, or is it instead
> a simple marking of lead?

Mr. Shaneyfelt: Yes. It is not a chip. There is no indication of any of the curbing having been removed, but rather it is a deposit of lead on the surface of the curbing that has given the appearance of a mark.

"It was also established from a microscopic study of the curbing that the lead object that struck the curbing, that caused the mark, was moving in a general direction away from the Texas School Book Depository building.

Mr. Redlich: In connection with this investigation into the microscopic characteristics of the mark, a photograph was prepared which is designated as Shaneyfelt Exhibit No. 35. Will you describe that photograph?"

(The photograph referred to was marked Shaneyfelt Exhibit No. 35 for identification.)

Mr. Shaneyfelt: Yes. Shaneyfelt Exhibit No. 35 is a color photograph that I made of the mark on the curbing, which is Shaneyfelt Exhibit No. 34. This is magnified about five times, and shows only the marked area. There is a red area in the lower left corner marked A which designates the point of initial impact, and the lead deposit is then sprayed out in a fan-like direction from that arrow."

Obviously, Shaneyfelt not only did not say what No-Source Posner attributed to him, he was quite careful not to say that. His testimony was also limited to a curbstone that had no "nick" or "hole" in it. There is no secret about the fact that it was in some mysterious way patched before Tague went to photograph it in May, 1964.

Shaneyfelt's testimony is secondhand or more distant from the one who did the testing and that was limited to "foreign metal smears." There was only one. It is those "smears" that the lab tested in this ghastly charade of police work or science, or of official investigations.

It is of them and of them only, not the impact of either a bullet or a fragment of a bullet, that Shaneyfelt gave his hearsay testimony when the man who did the testing was nearby if anybody wanted what the courts require, firsthand testimony.

Shaneyfelt gave the following descriptions of the result of that "test" that John F. Gallagher made: "determined to be essentially lead with a trace of antimony."

Of the origin Shaneyfelt testified not, as Posner represents, that it came from the core of the bullet Posner burdens with even more magic than the government did. Shaneyfelt testified that "the lead could have originated from the lead core of a mutilated metal-jacketed bullet *such as the type of bullet loaded into the 6.5 millimeter Mannlicher-Carcano cartridges, or from some other source having the same composition*." (The emphasis is added and the convoluted language is Shaneyfelt's.)

Although there was no question about it at all, the curbstone was, at the least, chipped, Shaneyfelt testified that what he had dug up and tested, "is not a chip." He added, his convoluted language again, "There is no indication of any of the curbing (sic) having been removed, but rather it is a deposit of lead on the surface of the curbing that has given the appearance of a mark."

He testified (hearsay), that "the object" that "caused the mark, was moving in a general direction away from the Texas School Book Depository Building." This is not on the lab records. They indicate the opposite. (*Post Mortem*, page 458.)

On that page I reproduced in facsimile Gallagher's own sketch, along with his own interpretation of the "results" of the spectrographic examination he made. In his sketch, what created what he referred to as a "smear" came from a 33-degree downward angle *from the west*! From the direction opposite to TSBD and its "sniper's nest"!

Posner did not have to examine any of my files to learn this. I reproduced it in facsimile in the book he had.

With regard to what caused that "smear," Gallagher's words, again in facsimile and on that same page, are "Small foreign metal smears (see attached for location) were run spectrographically (Jarrell-Ash) & found to be essentially lead with a trace of antimony—could be bullet metal. No copper observed."

"Jarrell-Ash" is the kind of spectrographic examination he made.

Note that Gallagher is careful not to say that the "smear" is bullet metal. He says only that it "could" be.

Posner's scholarship—and the alternative condemns him even more—is such that he believes and tells his readers that bullets are composed of only lead with only a "trace" of antimony. He should know better. And if he does know better and still tells his reader that there are only these two components of bullets to be detected when the examination is fine to parts per million and the various components of bullets are thoroughly mixed, what is he other than a determined, uninhibited perpetrator of a cruel fraud and that in his rewriting of the history of the assassination of a President?

He cannot have done any work on this subject without knowing the truth. And if he had not intended not telling the truth he would have recalled seeing, again in Gallagher's own handwriting and again in facsimile and again in *Post Mortem* and again in that same chapter (page 449) in Gallagher's tabulation of the third of his Jarrell-Ash spectrographic examination of four other lab bullet specimens that *the bullet in question is composed of 11 substances* all of which he has heading columns with their chemical symbols!

Aside from the fact that Shaneyfelt and Gallagher knew very well that "essentially lead with a trace of antimony" most certainly does *not* reflect a bullet, although knowing it they did imply it, they only *implied* it and *they did not say, as Posner represents*, that it *was* bullet residue that was disclosed by that test!

It was not!

When Shaneyfelt had that section of curbstone dug up he knew that there had been a chip in it and he had it dug up nonetheless. There is no reason to believe that the vaunted FBI knew that self-healing curbstones had been invented and were in use in Dallas!

There is no innocence in this for anyone involved in the investigation, especially not for Shaneyfelt. What he used to locate the precise spot, as he did, is from the official records in *Whitewash* (pages 158–9). He used the existing Dillard and Underwood pictures that long before Posner's formula became his book, before his twentieth birthday, I published in *Post Mortem*, which he has. (Page 608.)

While it was of no interest to Posner, those with an interest in these test results will find those that were disclosed in Part IV of *Post Mortem*.

It was not easy for the FBI to live by its own first and second "law," as many *former* agents have said, first "cover the bureau's ass" and then "cover your own ass" but with the necessary assistance of the Commission that lived in expressed terror of it, as its January 21, 1964, executive session transcripts disclose, (Post Mortem pp. 475 ff), *and the abject silence of all with guilty knowledge, it did and it got away with it and to this writing, continues to get away with it.*

The Dallas office rushed to cover its ass.

But maybe it would help to uncover Posner a bit more, with: the exception of the printed Commission testimony I use herein, each and every item was, and since before he passed his bar examination has been, in that "curbstone" file he ignored in the very files and file cabinets in which he spent most of his time here. And that, it should be remembered, was the month *after* he interviewed Tague.

One of these records, the one I cite next, has always been in that special file folder on my desk I direct everyone to, with Posner no exception. That is the Dallas FBI's ass-coverer.

Its then case agent was Robert P. Gemberling. When various reports were assembled into what the FBI calls "investigative reports" but actually consists of up to a thousand pages of such individual reports, Gemberling's was the major responsibility for doing that. For the "synopsis page" of the volume that included Shaneyfelt's cruel hoax, this is how Gemberling referred to it in his synopsis:

"Additional investigation conducted concerning mark on curb on south side of Main Street near triple underpass, which it is alleged was possibly caused by bullet during assassination. No evidence of mark or nick on curb now visible. Photographs taken of location *where mark once appeared.*" (emphasis added)

(The FBI had no monopoly on delays and creating evasive

records. Rankin, although he very obviously had been in touch
with the FBI much earlier, as the FBI's records reflect, did not
get around to sending the FBI Barefoot Sanders's assistant's
letter following his being cued in by Dillard until July 16! His
letter to Hoover says, without any explanation of any kind, that
he encloses the letter from Sanders's assistant, Martha J. Stroud,
"also enclosing the film referred to in this letter." He also
asked that the FBI "examine this film and advise us whether
it contains any additional information of probative value in connection with the assassination of President Kennedy." For all
anyone examining these records later could tell, Rankin could
have been interested in whether Kennedy had eaten something
that gave him a bellyache and that copies of the menu and of the
restaurant had been sent to him. Is it not necessary to wonder if
when bureaucrats go to all this kind of trouble to see to it that
their correspondence can mean nothing at all to anyone else
they have a reason for it? Rankin had, after all, been the government's lawyer for eight years. As solicitor general of the United
States he represented the United States before the Supreme
Court. Before which he surely dare no such goobledegook! But
when he was in charge of the Commission's investigation of
how Kennedy was killed, he found that appropriate for his incomprehensible goobledegook.")

After that I quote from Gemberling. He details the other pictures that were taken to make it appear that the original impact
came from that so-called "sniper's den" in the TSBD.

Gemberling, while less direct than he could and should have
been, made the ass-covering record that his office is not responsible for the grim charade because it reported that there had
been a "nick" on the curbstone and that when Shaneyfelt had
the city of Dallas dig that section up for him to fly to his lab
for its employment of the most advanced scientific testing, the
nick was no longer there.

Among the other FBI records in that "curbstone" file that
were of no interest to Posner—with the alternative no comfort
to him—is the "Laboratory Work Sheet." It reflects, among
other things of interest, the great dispatch with which the FBI
rushed. After the printed "Examination requested by" line, it

typed on "President's Commission (7–7–64)" which is only a month earlier!

After "Examinations requested" is typed "Photographic-Microscopic Firearms," the latter on the line below. It is encircled, reflecting that the copy is from that part of the lab. Above "Microscopic," "Spectrographic" is written in. The "date received" is 8–6–64. After "Examination by" only "Shaneyfelt" is typed in, and under his name "Frazier" is written in. Thus there is on this first page no identification of the spectrographer. That was Gallagher. Robert Frazier was a lab firearms examiner.

For those who may want to look further into this long-delayed but vital examination in my records, it is in the FBI headquarters "main" Oswald file, in the FBI's official file classifications list a "security-related" classification, it is "Foreign Counterintelligence" with "formerly Internal Security" of "nationalistic Tendency" among the other critical descriptions of it.) The FBI's file number for this Oswald file is 105–82555. Within that large file, this part of that testing is Serial 4668X. The file drawers reflect the serials each holds and the file folders identify the serials within each section, each single section or volume being in individual folders.

This page also has space at the bottom for comments to be added. Under "Specimen submitted for examination" it is typed, "Request for location and examination of mark on curbing at assassination site." The copy disclosed to me was made less understandable by repeated xeroxing. The size of Frazier's writing diminishing as he neared the end of the space available to him. In some places it is not legible at all.

Where what Frazier, the firearms not the spectrographic expert, wrote is legible, he does say that the results of the test, seemingly the encircled "firearms" examination but actually the spectrographic examination, show what he refers to as a "minor disturbance" on the "curb" at its "edge," meaning the rounded curbed edge where the horizontal and vertical surfaces join, can have been caused by "the core portion of a metal-jacketed bullet" like those allegedly used in the crime. But immediately after that he also gives as the possible cause, "a (sic) automobile weight or some other source of lead."

This is a lie, and it is a lie of such a nature that Frazier had to be sure there would not be any questioning of it.

It is a lie because Frazier knew that spectrographic examination disclosed only two of the 11 components of the bullet, or of the nine of its core.

But just imagine! He says it could have been caused not by a bullet but by the flying-off of one of the wheel weights with which automobile tires are balanced! Or something of similar composition.

This is to say it could have been caused by anything in the world composed of lead and antimony rather than a bullet!

(The FBI did not disclose this particular record and the Gemberling synopsis to me in my lawsuit for them and/or all other such records reflecting its scientific testing. It was disclosed under the compulsion of the later field offices lawsuits filed two years after I published *Post Mortem*.)

On the Frazier worksheet quoted above, alongside his drawing of the curbstone section showing that the portion tested was on the bend, with a line to the right and to his writing begins, "Partly discernable smoothing off–no groove or visible" and then it is not legible. It may refer to another form of mechanical injury or marking.

That "smoothing off" is something! Imagine a "firearms expert" examining a section of concrete curbstone that was known to have had a ballistics impact on it and that ballistic impact merely smoothed the concrete out more than it was when manufactured!

There is no question at all of what happened and as I set forth throughout *Post Mortem* Part IV, without a peep from the FBI then, since then, now more than a dozen years later, or at any point for the many years that test-result lawsuits were in court, where I alleged it under oath: *that curbstone was patched!*

This is clearly visible in the pictures. I first published them in *Post Mortem* on pages 608 and 609. On the left-hand page are the Underwood and Dillard pictures as of the time of the assassination and on the right-hand page is a picture of that curbstone section as it is in the Archives, this picture taken for me there. There is also an enlargement of that "smoothed-off" section. It is not only much smoother to sight and to touch, it is distinctly darker in shade.

This was more than merely visible to me—it was obvious. Is there any doubt that the FBI, meaning all the many involved in this charade in the FBI, including that ass-covering Gemberling in Dallas, had to know it even better than I? All those who made and filed reports, and who testified *under oath*?

When I, a nonexpert, was certain this was the case from those pictures and on reading Shaneyfelt's evasions and impossible testimony relating to any kind of bullet or bullet-fragment impact, were not all those FBI hotshots even more aware of it, more positive in what their education, training, and experience—all of them—knew?

Ought not all those Warren Commission counsels, especially the former assistant district attorney of Philadelphia, Arlen Specter, whose area of the Commission's work this was, have had at the very least a suspicion?

Not one said a word and among those who parlayed their Commission careers into professional advancements, Specter advanced until he is and has been a senator from Pennsylvania.

All combined in that awful crime of silence, when men ought to cry out!

Unlike the Posners who cringe at the mere thought of admitting that anybody had done any prior work in the area of their writing, I encourage others to use mine and I cannot remember asking to be credited a single time. Thus when Henry Hurt, a *Readers Digest* roving editor, a fine writer, an authentic conservative, and a southern gentleman of the old school, wrote *Reasonable Doubt*, (New York, Holt Rinehart and Winston, 1985) I gave him a free peer review of the manuscript as he wrote it. I urged him to carry my work on this evidence forward with what his publisher could afford and I could not, an expert examination of that piece of curbing resting in the Archives.

When we deposed John Kilty, another lab agent in that FOIA lawsuit for the test results* and the questioning turned to

---

*When I refiled that lawsuit under the amended FOIA as C.A.75-0226, the first case under the amended act, all the Lab agents involved, all relatively young, retired. Then the FBI claimed when I sought to depose them that

whether any test had been performed to determine whether there was a patch, he gave us some free advice in his answer:

"What you want to do is have a building-material scientist look at that. Different kinds of concrete that are used. They can tell the difference between a patching material and a permanent material. It's not a very difficult thing but you wouldn't use activation analysis to show it is different."

Remembering this I encouraged Henry and he took the FBI's professional advice, the advice of its famous laboratory. He did engage such a firm and under date of March 17, 1983, it reported to Henry's research assistant and fact-checker, Sissi Maleki. The "purpose" of his March 10 examination was "to look for external signs which might indicate that the concrete curbstone had been patched."

Naturally, Specter et al., including Posner, saw no such need. After all, it was merely the assassination of an American President they and the FBI were investigating and part of their responsibilities was to determine whether or not there had been a conspiracy. Oswald, long dead, had never had a free moment for patching that curbstone. Who had the motive to hide the evidence that "chip," also described as a "scar," held? The one and only thing accomplished by patching that innocent curbstone was to make it impossible to recover the metal deposits and analyze them scientifically. Doing that hid forever the traces of one of those bullets attributed to Oswald.

The only intent possible was to hide forever the composition of a bullet other than the one attributed to Oswald.

Here are excerpts from the report of the FBI-recommended professional examination:

because they had retired they could not be called to testify. The alleged reason was that they were no longer employed by the FBI. I had to litigate that before the court compelled them to appear and be deposed. Kilty replaced one of those who retired. He provided the FBI's affidavits. As soon as he started filing them, I proved he resorted to perjury. The response of that Judge John Pratt was to tell my lawyer, Jim Lesar and me first that we could catch more flies with honey than with vinegar and then that outside of court we could be sued for such statements. When Lesar offered to walk out of the courtroom and repeat the allegations, Pratt dropped the matter. And ignored Kilty's proven perjury.

At the center of the concrete curb section, on the vertical face just below the curbed transition between the horizontal and vertical surfaces, there was a dark gray spot. The dark spot had fairly well defined boundaries, so that it stood out visually from the surrounding concrete surface. The spot was roughly ellipsoidal in shape, approximately 1/2 in. by 3/4 in. in *principal dimensions.*

The surfaces of the curb which would normally have been exposed in service were visually examined with the aid of a 10X illuminated magnifier, with special attention given to the dark spot. It is significant to note that no other areas of any size were found anywhere on these surfaces with characteristics similar to those of the dark spot. These characteristics are described below.

The most obvious characteristic of the dark spot was the difference in color. The boundaries of the darker area were as well defined under the 10X magnifier as they were to the unaided eye. It is considered probably that the difference in color is due to the cement paste; however, the possibility of a surface-induced stain cannot be ruled out;.

Because the examination was limited to that curbstone as examined that day, this is a proper professional caution. But with there having been a visible damage, a "scar" or a "nick" or a "chip" that only a patch can explain it is obvious.

Another difference was noted in the color of the sand grains. The sand grains in the surrounding concrete surface were predominantly semi-translucent light gray in color, but there was also a significant amount of light brown sand grains. The dark spot contained only semi-translucent light grays and grains. It is possible that the difference in sand color may be due to a different kind of concrete; i.e., a patch, existing in the dark spot area. However, given the ratio of light gray sand grains to light brown sand grains in the surrounding concrete surface, and the relatively small size of the dark spot area, it is also possible that the difference in color of sand grains may be explained in terms of the statistical variations in the distribution of sand grains throughout the concrete mass.

The upper edge of the dark spot appeared to show marks of some sand grains having been dislodged along the boundary between the dark spot and the surrounding concrete area. This is consistent with the relatively weaker zones that normally occur in the thin, or "feathered," edges of a surface patch. Again, however, the dislodgement of sand grains could be due to other causes.

In summary, the dark spot shows visual characteristics which are significantly different from those of the surrounding concrete surface. While any one of the differences, by itself, could be easily explained in terms other than a patch, the simultaneous occurrence of those differences would amount to a rather curious coincidence of characteristics. But the existence of a surface patch would also be consistent with and explain all of the observed differences.

Because there had been the very visible mechanical damage at precisely that point there was no question remaining after the examination by a professional engineer from a respected firm of engineers. Not having the evidence of the damage before him, to eliminate any possible doubt he recommended . . . "that a more detailed visual examination, using techniques of microscopic petrograph, be conducted to gain more conclusive information regarding the cement paste, the sand grains and the surface coloration."

"Cement paste" is not what curbstones are cast of. They are of cast concrete.

What the FBI could tell me to do professionally and scientifically to determine the obvious it did not do for itself or the country. Naturally, its founding director already having had his vision from above and known before any investigation at all that Oswald was the assassin and the lone assassin. This in some detail in *Never Again!* that is being prepared for publication as I write this.

With what impaired vision and with the unaided eye—not even with a magnifying glass—it is that obvious—I could and did see was not visible to those upwardly mobile Commission legal eagles, Specter and all the others? Or to the FBI? Impossible!

This is the way that crime was investigated.

This is what left a fortune to be whored, what so disquieted and disenchanted so many, so many of whom were not then yet born.

This is what made it possible for the President to be consigned to history with the dubious epitaph of a dishonest noninvestigation that was officially decided upon virtually the instant Oswald died, as is documented in *Never Again!*

The engineering report, too, was in the "Curbstone" file Posner either did not look at or looked in and ignored a full month after his two days with Tague.

And this is, too, only one of the many reasons Posner and his ilk should be consigned to history's refuse heaps.

IX
The Model of Historical Scholarship

The last words in Posner's book are like those of a prosecutor closing his case:

> *"Lee Harvey Oswald, driven by his own twisted and impenetrable furies, was the only assassin at Dealey Plaza on November 22, 1963. To say otherwise, in light of the overwhelming evidence, is to absolve a man with blood on his hands, and to mock the President he killed."* (Page 472.)

Had this been in a court of law rather than of public opinion; had Oswald ever had a defense counsel prepared to give him a vigorous defense, what Posner says in closing and what he says throughout would have been subjected to a much more rigorous examination than is possible for an unwell and partly handicapped octogenarian who has to depend on his memory and lacks meaningful access to his own materials.

But with no more than memory retrieved, Posner's prosecution-type case would not have survived before a real jury. None of it stacks, not a single solitary bit of evidence of the crime itself. His Hartsogian shrinkery, meaning what Posner said it meant when it means no such thing, might have had no basis at all before the court because Hartsog would have had to deliver it. Posner and he then would have been horned by the dilemma; present him and risk having his sex-with-Hartogs therapy for women patients before the jury which would have had to evaluate his testimony as coming from him, with his record and to this add that Hartogs himself swore the opposite of the basis of Posner's book, or not run that risk, not present him at all.

Without Hartogs, Prosecutor Posner has none of those "furies" he imagined to impute to Oswald.

Without that he has no motive to attribute to Oswald. The prosecutor then has a crime without any motive at all rather than a trial with a motive he made up with no more basis than his interpretation of what Hartogs meant in what he said about Oswald as a troubled boy.

Posner did not even deny it when face-to-face with my friend Dr. Cyril Wecht, who is both a lawyer and a forensic pathologist, on CNN, September 3, 1993, Wecht said to him that his book was only "a prosecutor's brief."

Not only does Posner give no other side, he pretends there is none, save with what he picks and chooses, not always faithfully, from the trash of the theorized conspiracies. In his dishonest version there is no other defense and only what he says is factual and relevant when it is neither.

Without a defense lawyer and judge to keep him honest, Posner was not honest.

In a court of law he would have been lampooned from beginning to end for his ignorance of what he talks about and for his not uncommon outright lies.

We can say as a defense counsel would have said, "Counselor, you have sprayed a deodorant on the same old garbage and it still stinks."

That is all that Posner did and with two exceptions; it is not more than that same old garbage and nothing else since my first book exposed it for what it is—almost thirty years ago.

As we have seen, and what I have used is not by any means all the illustrations of it, even those 200 interviews Posner brags so about were not intended to yield any new evidence—they yielded none, either—and what is left is Posner's inaccurate and undependable pretense that the deodorant makes that old garbage smell like roses when it is in fact only the very same malodorous garbage.

Those interviews were no more than a trick to be able to pretend they hold what is new and relevant when they do not at all. They were his means of avoiding the truth. In court, some of his cherished sources would have been disastrous to him; those of the ilk of Alexander, Bringuier, and Badeaux. Examples of those misused to hide what is already public through his suppressive interviews of them are Yosenko and Tague.

Examination of it with less skill and resources than a defense counsel would have shown it to be totally flawed. It distorts it, misrepresents it, and is often based on ignorance. It is factually incorrect and it is dishonest in many ways.

In court that would be ruinous, as before the court of public opinion it will be.

In the future a longer and more detailed version of this work will be available for scholars of the future to consult. Contact: David Wrone, Professor of History, University of Wisconsin; Gerald McKnight, Hood College, Frederick, MD; or Harold Weisberg at 7627 Old Receiver Road, Frederick, MD 21702

Conclusion

This book is, as intended, an exposure and an indictment of Gerald Posner and his mistitled book, *Case Closed,* the most dishonest of all the many books on the assassination of President Kennedy and its investigations. It also exposes and indicts the media and those who connived with Posner.

How dishonest are Posner and his book? Strong as is the case in this book, it is much less than the case I put together and that was much less than was possible. By the time my manuscript exceeded more than 200,000 words I did no more. This book shortens that lengthy indictment to make it more accessible to more people. However, copies of that lengthier indictment will be deposited with professional historians and their institutions for the historical record for the future. These historians provided the professional peer review that Posner and Random House avoided. They avoided this tradition on non-fiction publication for a very simple reason: with a competent peer review they would have had no such successful exploitation and commercialization of this great tragedy in our history.

Despite the prepublication raves by men of eminence not one of whom was in a position to offer the opinions used to sell this rewriting of our history. The professional historian among them, Stephen Ambrose, was silent when I wrote him. He has no defense of what he did. I asked that of him.

Posner is a man, as the full manuscript proves much more than this book does, who has trouble telling the truth even by accident.

This extends even to himself. He was not a Wall Street lawyer. His actual "Wall Street" experience was a short span of the most insignificant and most menial work, on "discovery" material for IBM in a major anti-trust case.

Without any of the media making any check at all, it, too, puffed him up as what he was and is not, a "Wall Street lawyer."

Of the innumerable instances of his subject-matter ignorance, I cite one.

I select this one because he had access to the fact in two ways. The first is that I published it in my 1965 book of which he has a copy and to which he refers in his book. His reading of that book was so close that he quoted four non-continuous words from a page of about 600 words. The other is that I have a file on it and he had unsupervised access to all my some 60 file cabinets of records and to our copier.

In support of his nonexisting case of a shot fired in the assassination earlier than the Commission said he refers to the late Nobel Laureate Luis Alvarez as the inventor of the "jiggle" theory, that amateur photographer Abraham Zapruder's reaction to an earlier shot caused his camera to jiggle. I brought that to light in my 1965 *Whitewash*. Alvarez's students then asked him about this. He later wrote an article about it and had it published in *The Scientific American*—which Posner does not mention. My file, which is not included in the FOIA lawsuit to which I refer earlier in this book because I did not have to take that one to court, includes even Alvarez contemptuous disregard for his misuse of funds provided by the Energy Research and Development Administration for that work and publication.

But then Posner did not dare cite either my first use of that Zapruder testimony or the testimony itself because what Zapruder actually testified to is that a shot had come from behind him, from that Grassy Knoll so infamous to Posner, and that he saw the President hit by the first shot fired, earlier than in the first of the official account! The shot that Posner said missed. (*Whitewash,* page 47)

There are few people bolder than Posner in his dishonesty, few who respond to criticism by making personal attacks on those who criticize him more than he does.

One of the many illustrations of this is when Dr. Cyril Wecht, to Posner's face on CNN, said that Posner had used Failure Analysis's work as his own. Posner launched a false and a personal, attack on Wecht instead of addressing the obvious truth Wecht spoke. That was, as Wecht soon proved, a false attack—another Posner lie. But in responding to Posner's false attack Wecht used up all the time, Posner got away with it and was even able to add to his lies that Wecht had "distorted" in telling the literal truth.

Posner got away with the same thing in a letter to the Washington *Post*'s weekly Book World section. In a perceptive review, reporter Jeffrey Frank had noted the same factual and truthful criticism that Posner used Failure Analysis' work as his or for him. Here is Posner's response, which is not only not a response but is a carefully-designed lie: the *Post* accommodated him by publishing it in its December 12, 1993 issue:

"The insinuation that I claimed that FAA's enhancements were commissioned for the book is false. In the book, the citations to FAA's work and Dr. Piziali's testimony refer to the 1992 ABA mock trial which is a matter of public record."

In this Posner intended to lie, having no real choice.

There is no mention in his book of the American Bar Association or its mock trial or of "testimony" there by Piziali!

If Posner had mentioned any of that he could not have gotten away with his studied pretense that all that work was for him. That the mock trial was a matter of public record is irrelevant. Posner's shyster-like reference to it here is to say that he told all of that in his book, which he did not.

Had he, he would have exposed himself and his book and he would have killed it in the writing.

He is clever at such deceptions and his practise of them never ends.

His and his publisher's claim is that the most important part of his book is his biography of Oswald. It is contrived to make it appear that there is a factual basis for Posner's saying he was a born assassin. Posner says this based on what he says is the professional opinion of the New York City psychiatrist, Dr. Renatus Hartogs. Hartogs examined Oswald when he was an unhappy little boy who behaved badly. But in fact, when a witness before the Warren Commission and at precisely the very point in his testimony Posner cites repeatedly, Hartogs swore to the exact opposite!

Posner begins his book with his fabrication that Oswald was that born assassin. At the very outset, in carrying this fiction forward, he says that Oswald was so pleased with himself after assassinating the President that he "smirked" repeatedly. Posner repeatedly, says that using that work twice, on page 4 alone, for example.

I checked all Posner's sources out. Like Renatus, Posner cites their Warren Commission testimony. *Not one of his claimed sources used that word or even suggested it!*

Posner lied and the ever unquestioning media went for it. And has yet to expose him. Which would mean, of course, expose itself. Not very likely.

When this is so very blatant on the most cursory check, what does this say about the media which did no checking at all and made him a world-famous man as soon as his fraud of a book was out? What does it tell us of the degree to which we can depend on our media, the means by which we are informed so that we can meet our responsibilities in a representative society.

It tell us that the media more than retails it. It glorifies liars. How, then, can the public be truthfully informed? How can our system work? The KGB suspected Oswald might be an American agent. At least some should have known that the first Commission crisis was when it could no longer avoid such a report. It is, among other public sources, in Gerald Ford's book. He had been a Commission Member and the House Republican leader. A telephone call to any of the many critics familiar with it or to me would have disclosed that I had published the fact that Oswald had a Top Secret and a Crypto clearance when he was a Marine. *That* kind of high security clearance for a man later accused of assassinating the President and that Commission did not report it? And Posner's book, for all its emphasis on its account of Oswald and his career makes no mention of it?

The media itself changed with its universal acceptance of the official assassination mythology. Instead of giving that Report the critical analysis we expect of it, the media rivaled in glorifying it when in fact the Report alone cannot survive critical examination and when compared with its supposed evidentiary base in those 26 volumes it is clearly a work not of inquiry but of politically sought "truth" that is not true.

Our society can work as intended by our Founding Fathers, ✗ those who to me were the greatest political thinkers in history, only when the people are informed truthfully and accurately. That can happen only when the media tells them the truth, reports fact not falsehood as it did with Posner and his mistitled book.

As this fraction of what I was able to write in a mere two months reflects, neither Posner nor his book can survive critical examination.

He knew about it because he had and read my *Oswald in New Orleans,* which reported it in 1967. That was the only one of my books he had when he bought the others from me. It is also the book based on a minor fact in it he attributed his only factual error to me. He did not know what he was talking about because what he criticized is correct and his criticism was so obviously wrong he could have learned that from the phone book. It is an address.

When he appeared while promoting his book soon after it was out at the Green Apples book store in his home town of San Francisco, my friend Hal Verb asked him why that book is not in his bibliography. Posner's response is that his bibliography lists only the books he used!

Hal knew that was a lie, as did other of my friends who were there.

But with Posner's mother also there, none wanted to embarrass him by proving him a liar to his mother's face and that in public.

There is no question about it, Posner knew that Oswald did have that exceptionally high security clearance and that it was expunged from his Marines record. We even discussed it when he was here.

Posner knew that Oswald had that exceptional security clearance. But he could not have reported that in his book that makes Oswald the lone assassin. That is the same reason it is expunged from Oswald's Marines records.

(I have since made those records available to John Newman who is writing a book based on the Oswald records suppressed until their disclosure was compelled by law in 1993.)

That in time of great crisis and with this assassination, ever since then, all of our institutions failed and continue to fail us and themselves is the thrust of my work. This book is the eighth of my published books in which this failure is brought to light, with a ninth to be published later this year. That and all those FOIA lawsuits and their yield, in court precedents and in that third of a million pages of now available and previously-withheld official records is not an inconsiderable work.

Yet not a single reporter writing about Posner and his book, not a single news magazine that promoted it, not a single TV show or ostensible news account asked me a single question about that book for all the work I have done and am known to have done in the field.

In the entire country, with this the subject and with Posner's version of that great tragedy, not one reporter who wrote any story at all about it asked a single question!

This describes our media today better and more definitively than any critic of it can.

Book publishing is, of course, an important element of our media. While a book does not reach the audience of the print press or the electronic media, it is the one means by which important national issues can be addressed at length and with real definitiveness.

But not a single major publisher has brought out a single truthful, responsible book that is critical of the government's record when the President was killed, when as is inevitable, we had an American *coup d'etat.*

If any believe that was not the effect of this assassination, they need only compare our country and life in it then with what we have today. After Viet Nam, after the Watergate, after the Iran/Contra disgrace, after a President was forced to resign rather than be impeached, after he picked his successor who then immediately pardoned him.

Crime is a major national issue. Compare crime now with then, with 30 years ago.

Look at the streets overflowing with the homeless, many of whom had decent jobs and could not afford a place to live despite being employed. Was this true then?

The national debt is another major issue. Compare it now with what it was then.

Compare what we now have to import that we used to export, daily increasing the national debt thereby, with that national debt alone denying the country its urgent needs.

Compare our infant mortality then and now and with that all the other major health problems. For a developed country we now have one of the highest infant mortality rates.

There is no real question, the assassination of a President in our country inevitably had the greatest consequences. It also nullifies our entire system of government. It is the greatest subversion.

Yet the major media failed to meet its responsibilities then and ever since then and as this book shows, persists in refusing to meet its responsibilities after 30 years.

No major book publisher has ever published this kind of criticism—and it is constructive criticism in a society like ours—and when such a book can be published, it is by a small publisher. They have the courage.

We are in bad shape when this can happen in our country. *And it has happened!*

When the Posners can get the Random Houses to publish such malevolent, such dangerous trash as his mistitled *Case Closed,* the title he knew and admitted is untrue, when the major media can fall all over itself in telling the people that such a crude lie is the truth, when this is what happens when our government fails—*and it did happen*—then we are all in danger with our system in such great trouble.

As the philosopher Santayana observed so succintly and truthfully, those who do not remember the past are doomed to relive it.

We *are* reliving it. We'd better remember!